How can I get myself to do what I need to do?

Terry Gogna

How can I get myself to do what I need to do?

By Terry Gogna

Copyright © 2007 Terry Gogna

Edited by Anil Gogna & Catherine Nanton

Printed in Canada
First Edition, Nov 2007

ISBN: 978-1-897518-05-2

To order more copies of this book:
www.pemsystem.com
Tel: 1 866 535 1352

BOOK DESIGN AND LAYOUT

N-VISAGE
MEDIA.COM

T +44 (0)121 240 3579 E info@n-visagemedia.com W www.n-visagemedia.com

Why I Wrote This Book

As an Entrepreneur and Personal Success Coach, I have come across many people over the years who have shared their dreams with me.

They have been open to me about the special things they want to accomplish in their lives: What they want to provide for their family, the charities they want to help, the places around the world they want to visit, the things they want to do to help their church and the beautiful future they want to create for themselves & their families.

They talk about their dreams like little children at Christmas, filled with so much anticipation and excitement, *dying* to open their pile of presents hidden away under the Christmas tree.

It makes me sad that so many of the adults I have coached approach life the same way. They believe that in order to achieve success, all they have to do is reach for the gift and open it. Like naïve little children, they expect no struggle and end up unprepared.

When struggles come, and they always will, many people assume that they are on the wrong road and quit. I don't believe that these people have given up on their dreams. However, I do believe they are simply looking for an easier road, one without potholes; no struggles along the way.

This book is my message to people around the world who have a dream to do something great with their lives.

Every road that leads to the fulfillment of your dream will be filled with potholes – struggles you cannot avoid. You must accept the fact that the struggles on the road are simply the "chisel-cuts" of life, sculpting you into the great person you can be, as long as you stay on the road.

When the struggles come, don't walk away. Instead, lean into them and be prepared to "take-the-hit." Every time you get hit, it is simply a sign telling you, "it is time for you to look inside yourself and make some adjustments." It is not a sign for you to quit.

This book is all about those little adjustments that you may need to make along your journey.

By the way, I'd love to hear about how this book has helped you in your personal journey towards accomplishing your dreams. I'm sure your story will inspire all who read it. Looking forward to your e-mail,

Terry Gogna

Terry Gogna FT.FHS
TerryGogna@pemsystem.com

Dedication and Acknowledgements

I would like to dedicate this book to three very special groups of people:

First:
To God, my parents, my wife & best friend, Rani and my two sons, Anil and Aaron... I am not a self-made person; I am who I am because of those who have supported and challenged me. Thank you all.

Second:
To all the very special individuals around the world that have experienced tremendous pain and struggle in their lives, yet did not give up on their dreams no matter how painful their journey became. Your journey of pain and tears has given hope and strength to many others. Even though YOU may not be aware of it personally, GOD is. Thank you for inspiring us all to chase our passions, by "staying the course" and not giving up on your dreams.

Third:
To my Heroes; tired, discouraged, betrayed, heartbroken and persecuted... you did not give up and abandon your missions. Thank you for showing me the way.

Contents

Introduction - There Is No Such Thing As "Time Management"   1

Chapter 1 - The "Hidden" Principle Of Success   5

Chapter 2 - Getting Started With The "P.E.M. System"   17

Chapter 3 - Inputting Data Into The "P.E.M. System"   23

Chapter 4 - Slay Or Sleep With Your "Giant"   31

Chapter 5 - There Is ALWAYS Time For EVERY Important
Thing In Your Life   39

Chapter 6 - You Are In A War And The Battleground Is
Inside Your Head   49

Chapter 7 - Self Discovery   57

Chapter 8 - It's All About The "Results"   61

Chapter 9 - The "Layout" Of Your Day   69

Chapter 10 - "P.E.M. System Tips" For Sales Professionals   75

Chapter 11 - Create Your Own Personal "Success Environment"   87

Chapter 12 - There Is No Such Thing As A Secure Job
Or Business, There Are Only "Secure" People   117

Conclusion - Wisdom Is The "Application" Of Knowledge   171

There Is No Such Thing As "Time Management"

> *"We must not allow the clock and the calendar to blind us to the fact that each moment of life is a miracle and mystery."*
>
> - H. G. WELLS

How often have you heard the phrases: "I don't have time" or "I have to make time?"… I know what you're thinking, "I just said that today." We've all heard these words so often that we never take the time to listen to what we're actually saying.

We hear and use these words so frequently that we never question their accuracy. Instead we convince ourselves, without a doubt, of their truth. I want to make a point here and now:

You cannot "make" or "manage" TIME. You can only create and manage **personal events**.

"Know the true value of time; snatch, seize, and enjoy every moment of it. No idleness, no laziness; no procrastination; never put off till tomorrow what you can do today."

- LORD CHESTERFIELD

Webster's dictionary says, "To manage something is to 'handle,' 'direct' or 'alter' something for a purpose." You cannot manage time because you cannot handle, direct or alter time for any purpose. You cannot speed up time and you cannot slow time down.

You can only control and manage the events that you personally carry out in the time that already exists.

So, the next time you hear the words, "Time Management," remember, there is no such thing as "Time Management."

"Event Management" is the only way to successfully *pretend* that you are actually managing time.

By the way, organizing your daily events in segments of 15 minutes or less throughout the whole day will give you the *perception* that you are actually capturing and slowing time down.

The **Priority Event Management System** is a tool that will enable you to effectively organize and elevate your "Personal and Professional Success" through a process of understanding and prioritizing the events you carry out on a daily basis.

Throughout this book, I will be referring to the "Priority Event Management System" as the **P.E.M. System**.

"One should count each day a separate life."

- SENECA

Chapter 1

The "Hidden" Principle Of Success

"Beware the barrenness of a busy life."

- SOCRATES

It is common knowledge that there are success principles that, when followed diligently, yield great success in any area of our lives. So why is it that so many people who have achieved obvious and significant success in ONE area of their life lack significant success in other areas of their life?

If we truly knew how it was that we became successful in one particular area, would we not want to apply those same principles to all the other areas of our life?

We would be right in saying that if we are significantly successful in one area of our life and significantly NOT successful in other areas, then we either:

"Real knowledge is to know the extent of one's ignorance."

- CONFUCIUS

1. Don't care about being successful in those other areas of our life.

2. Have accepted the false truth that, "In order to achieve significant success in any one area of life, we MUST sacrifice all other areas of our life."

3. Perhaps we don't really know exactly how we became successful in that one area. There may be other principles of success in action **behind the scenes**, of which we are simply not aware, apart from the obvious ones that have caused our success such as passion, determination, perseverance and focus of consistent effort.

If we assume that the real reason is point number three, what other possible principles of success are in action behind the scenes?... Ones of which we are not aware of or that we refuse to pay attention to.

On a daily basis, there are two types of "events/activities," that we all engage in: **Present-Based** events & **Future-Based** Events.

Present-Based events allow us to maintain a certain level of comfort and happiness in our life. However, no matter how much time and dedication we put into these events, they will not cause any SIGNIFICANT change in our present life or lifestyle. These Present-Based events **alone**, will not create a new and better future significantly different from the one we currently experience.

Two Examples:

1. No matter how much time we put into cleaning our house, the house cleaning event will not move us to a nicer home in the future. It will only keep our present home clean.

2. Reading positive mental attitude books will almost always makes us feel good about the possibilities of a better future. However, no matter how much we read, our future will never differ from our present until we apply what we've learned from our reading and actually do something that will directly create a different future.

"The future depends on what we do in the present."

- MOHANDAS GANDHI

Future-Based events are the source of change in our life and lifestyle; they create our new and better future. However, unless we know exactly why we are engaged in this type of an event, we can easily get discouraged to the brink of quitting. When we engage in a Future-Based event, immediate results are often not seen. The results of Future-Based events "show up" in the future.

Two Examples:

1. People who weight train don't expect to look and feel great the same day they work out. Quite the contrary; the exhaustion and aches experienced after weight training often last a day or two. People choose to go through the pain and struggle of working out so they can look forward to feeling and looking great in the near future.

2. Sales people can listen to motivational CDs and practice their presentation all day long, but until they pick up the phone and contact somebody about their product or business they will never create a future that is different from their present; they will only continue to experience what they presently have in the future.

If we busy ourselves all day long with ONLY Present-Based events, we will be guaranteeing our future lifestyle to look exactly like the one we currently have in the present.

The key to success lies in truly understanding and differentiating between a Present-Based and a Future-Based event.

When making a list of Present-Based and Future-Based events, we may be uncertain whether an event is Present-Based or Future-Based because either could be justified. The deciding factor will be based on the actual goals we have set for ourselves in the different areas of our lives. We first need to know exactly what we want to achieve in the future, so we can then set up a game plan to achieve it.

The purpose of the following exercise is not to gather a "big as possible" list of important things that create our future, but to **discover the most important SINGLE EVENT that will either make or break our future in EACH particular area of our life.** It is absolutely crucial that we identify this "one event."

> *"If a man does not know to what port he is steering, no wind is favourable to him."*
>
> - SENECA

9

"Never leave that till tomorrow, which you can do today."

- BENJAMIN FRANKLIN

The simplest way to differentiate whether or not an event is Present-Based or Future-Based is to ask ourselves, "If I only do this one event and nothing else, could I achieve my future goal?"

No matter how strongly we feel that more than one activity needs to be done to achieve a particular future goal, the key still lies in identifying only ONE "root event" which is greater than all of the others, when it comes to creating our desired future.

Three Examples:

1. In order to achieve my future goal of being fit and healthy, I must carry out the following events:

- Eat healthy foods
- Eat 5 to 6 smaller meals
- Exercise regularly

In this example, if we eat healthy foods in smaller meals but leave out exercise, we may become healthier but we are not going to improve our overall fitness level. Exercising is therefore the "root event" that will cause the greatest change to our present life/lifestyle, which will then help us to achieve our desired future. Exercise is the Future-Based event; the other two are Present-Based events.

2. In order to be successful in my business, I must carry out the following events:

- Listen to motivational and
  educational CDs
- Read personal growth books
- Attend seminars
- Make prospecting calls (contacts)
- Deliver presentations

First, if we only listen to CDs or only read books or only attend seminars, we will never achieve our desired future because we are only "getting ready" to act.

Second, if we have no appointments to show our business presentations or products to prospects, we will never achieve our desired future. Therefore, "making contacts" becomes the Future-Based "root event" and everything else becomes Present-Based.

"You can't build a reputation on what you are going to do."

- HENRY FORD

> *"Most people would succeed in small things if they were not troubled with great ambitions."*
>
> - Henry Wadsworth Longfellow

3. "I work so hard on my school work yet I don't understand why I'm not getting the grades."

There are many students who are actually convinced that they are working very hard at their school work. However, if you examine their activities, the reason they are not getting the grades they want is obvious to the observer, yet the students who are emotionally involved in their "studying" are totally oblivious. Here's what I mean:

In a regular four hour study session here's a list of all the things this student was actually doing:

1. Getting clothes ready for the next day

2. Cleaning up their desk and bedroom

3. Organizing their school bag

4. Organizing laptop computer files

5. Emailing friends

6. "MSN-ing" friends

7. Receiving incoming calls from friends

8. Re-writing notes over and over because they were not neat enough

9. Memorizing formulas

10. **Actually studying by trying to understand relevant content**

This student subconsciously concluded that because he went into his room at 6:00pm and came out of his room at 10:00pm, he studied for four hours. Any "time" that he spent on any of the tasks listed above between 6:00pm and 10:00pm was all part of his "studying hard" program. However, this student needs to understand that event number ten is the ONLY Future-Based event that will create his "desired future" of better grades. All of the other nine events are Present-Based; they are not the direct "root cause" of better grades.

No matter how good this student is at all of the other nine events, if he leaves out event number ten, he will surely fail. This student should be doing event number ten first, before any of the other activities.

"In all things success depends on previous preparation and without such previous preparation there is sure to be failure."

- CONFUCIUS

"Everything that looks to the future elevates human nature; for never is life so low or so like, as when occupied with the present."

- WALTER SAVAGE LANDOR

In conclusion, until we identify the significant Future-Based events in each area of our lives and understand their INCREDIBLE POWER and VALUE in changing our present life/lifestyle, we will continue to fill our days with events that hinder our future and cause no change in our present lives. And in the coming days and nights, like so many others, we will wonder why our lives are not changing despite all our hard work.

The "Hidden" Principle Of Success:

All events are either Present-Based or Future-Based; they will either take you to your future or keep you in the present.

Make sure you are on the right "bus."

Look out of the window. Is the scenery changing, or is your bus (your life) going around in circles?

If it's not changing, get off the bus. Just because you're moving (working hard and staying busy) doesn't mean you are heading to the right place.

Only the right bus will take you to the right place.

Only Future-Based events will create your desired future.

The "hidden" principle of success is now no longer "hidden" as far as you, the reader, is concerned. The only question that remains is, "Will you ignore this discovery, or will you take advantage of it?"

"The great thing in this world is not so much where you stand, as in what direction you are moving."

- OLIVER WENDELL HOLMES

Chapter 2

Getting Started With The "P.E.M. System"

To get started with the P.E.M. System, we first need to list the different events/activities that we currently carry out on a regular basis.

An "event" is any activity that you do or would like to make time for, regardless of how long it takes to carry out.

As you begin to make your list, you will be tempted to include other events which you are not currently doing but would like to do. DON'T BE TEMPTED! List ONLY the things you are currently doing on a daily, weekly and monthly basis.

*"He that can
have patience
can have what
he will."*

- BENJAMIN FRANKLIN

You can add more things to the P.E.M. System gradually as you get more comfortable with the process. So, on a separate piece of paper go ahead and list your events.

Here are some suggestions that may help to jog your memory:

Health
Meals – Breakfast, Lunch, Dinner
Exercise

Spiritual
Church
Prayer time
Volunteer work

Personal
Reading affirmations
Hobbies - reading, learning language, dance, painting, music, sports, etc
Grocery shopping
Mowing the lawn
Cleaning house
Laundry
Walking the dog
Paperwork
TV

Financial
Place of work (Job or business)
Higher education - studying at night to
    increase level of job (e.g. MBA)
Part-time business building activities:
    Prospecting calls, listening to
    motivational and educational CDs,
    reading books, attending seminars,
    delivering presentations

Relationships
Parents
Spouse
Children
Family time

After you have completed your list, identify the Future-Based events ONLY. All others will automatically be Present-Based events. Remember, Future-Based events are the ONLY events that can and do create change in your present life/lifestyle and create a new and better future.

The example below shows the same list but now the Future-Based events have been highlighted in **bold text:**

Health
Meals – Breakfast, Lunch, Dinner
Exercise

"You should not live one way in private and another in public."

- PUBLILIUS SYRUS

Spiritual
Church
Prayer time
Volunteer work

Personal
Reading affirmations
Hobbies - reading, learning language, dance, painting, music, sports, etc
Grocery shopping
Mowing the lawn
Cleaning house
Laundry
Walking the dog
Paperwork
TV

Financial
Place of work (Job or business)
Higher education - **studying at night to increase level of job (e.g. MBA)**
Part-time business building activities: **Prospecting calls,** listening to motivational and educational CDs, reading books, attending seminars, delivering presentations

Relationships
Parents
Spouse
Children
Family time

Now that you have created your list of events and identified those that are Future-Based in each area of your life, you are ready to input them into the **"P.E.M. System Daily Template"** pictured below.

"Employ thy time well, if thou meanest to get leisure."

- BENJAMIN FRANKLIN

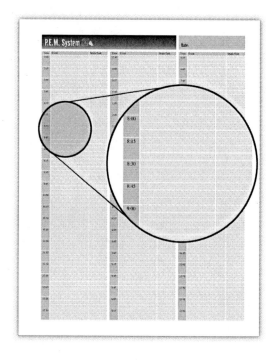

The above "Daily Templates" are included in the **"P.E.M. System Planner."** Planners can be purchased online at: **www.pemsystem.com**

Chapter 3

Inputting Data Into The "P.E.M. System"

> *"He who has begun has half done. Dare to be wise; begin."*
>
> - HORACE

Before you start inputting data into the P.E.M. System you need to have the correct mindset. If you have the mindset of a perfectionist, expecting to have everything correctly inputted on your first attempt, you will get very frustrated.

Understand that this is an **evolving process of self-discovery.** You will be learning many things about yourself and how you really operate on a daily basis.

As you continue to use the P.E.M. System you will need to constantly make minor adjustments on a daily basis, so be prepared to do so.

Other than Future-Based & Present-Based Events there are two more very

"He who every morning plans the transaction of the day and follows out that plan, carries a thread that will guide him through the maze of the most busy life. But where no plan is laid, where the disposal of time is surrendered merely to the chance of incidence, chaos will soon reign."

- VICTOR HUGO

important types of events that we need to cover here: **"Fixed"** and **"Flexible"** Events.

Fixed Events include events such as going to work. Here you have no flexibility. You must leave your home at a specific time in order to get to work, stay there for a period of time and then leave at a certain time.

The only flexibility most people may have during work is at lunch time and that depends on how much time they have for lunch. A half-hour lunch doesn't leave much time for anything else except eating. However, a one hour lunch may provide some flexibility to do other things.

Another example of a Fixed Event may be to walk your dog at 7:00am every morning. This is a fixed event because otherwise he'll poop in your house!

For the current week only, go ahead and input your Fixed Events into your "P.E.M. System Planner."

Here's an example of a template with ONLY "Fixed" events inputted:

Daily Template Showing "Fixed" Events ONLY

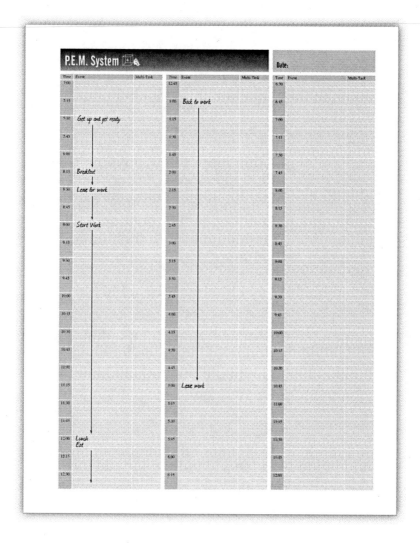

All the blank space that you see in the template, is referred to as "Flexible" time. **What you choose to do in it will determine your future.**

Now go ahead and input ONLY your Future-Based Events into each template for the next seven days. How much of a particular event you carry out in a day is up to you. It's YOUR future.

After only a few days of using the "P.E.M. System," most people are absolutely shocked to see how much of their daily life was actually being wasted on events that did absolutely nothing for their future.

The secret to why the P.E.M. System works so well is that it focuses you on what's important first. **Always input first, that which creates your future,** then fit everything else into the rest of the time available.

Now input your Present-Based events into either the time slots remaining or into the multi-tasking columns. Do this for the next seven days also. It's not as easy as you may think it is. It will take some organizing and a lot of patience, but it will be well worth it in the long run.

There will be many times when you feel that there just isn't enough time in a day to fit in all the events that you would like to do. When you feel this way, you must understand, you do not have to stick to the "norm" of daily, weekly, and monthly events. Begin first by listing everything that you'd like to make time for and then allocate appropriate time to each of the events depending on their priority level.

"A clever person solves a problem, a wise person avoids it."

- ALBERT EINSTEIN

For example, you can do an event every other day, weekly, every ten days, bi-weekly or monthly. This way you are still able to carry out the event and not feel guilty that you're not making time for it.

There will also be special activities that you would really like to do such as painting, writing songs or practising the piano. However, you rarely make time to do these things because when you do, you feel guilty that you're wasting time on something that is not going to better your future, even though these particular activities make you feel really good and actually energize you!

"Success is not the key to happiness. Happiness is the key to success. If you love what you are doing, you will be successful."

- ALBERT SCHWEITZER

Make sure that you put these kinds of events into your P.E.M. System and engage in them even if it's only once a month. At least you'll feel great that you're doing something that you love to do.

You have to always make time for the little things that make you feel good and give you peace. Doing them will uplift your spirits and help you to become more effective and productive in everything else you do. Carrying out these special events will also make you a better person to be around.

About a year ago, I was reading a book that was focused on the subject of "hidden passions and fading dreams." The author was saying that so many people live their lives without ever doing what they really want to. They never make time for the things that they are passionate about. He suggested that you ask your spouse what they really like doing for fun; what makes them happy? Then when they tell you, make sure you make the time to do it with them because this is what will bring joy into your relationship.

I decided I was going to do it, but before asking my wife, I tried to guess what I thought she would say; I guessed, "dancing." Then I asked her. She said, "Salsa dancing, why are you asking?" I said, "Oh, I was just curious." As I walked away from her, I began to realize how much of an idiot I had been for asking her. I hate dancing! I started to feel sick. I knew I shouldn't have asked her, especially when I knew what she was going to say. How stupid was that? Now I had a decision to make. Am I going to contribute to my wife's happiness by taking salsa classes with her, or just ignore what she said?

I couldn't ignore it. I mean, what kind of husband would I be especially now that I know what makes her happy. So I booked us both in for salsa classes. When I told her, she began to "freak out," in good way.

At our first class I couldn't believe the look on her face; the joy in her eyes was priceless as she got on the dance floor.

I thought to myself, what kind of husband would I be to hold back the very thing that would give my wife so much pleasure. By the way, our dance classes

"Each friend represents a world in us, a world possibly not born until they arrive, and it is only by this meeting that a new world is born."

- ANAIS NIN

29

"The man least dependent upon the morrow goes to meet the morrow most cheerfully."

- Epicurus

are now in my P.E.M. System as a weekly Fixed Event; dancing turned out to be quite fun and not as "scary" as I thought it would be.

By the way, it is very important that you schedule as many of the events of each day, ahead of time, preferably a week in advance. If you find yourself filling in your P.E.M. System template on the morning of a particular day, your scheduling for the day will be swayed by your "mood of the moment" and you will not be as productive as you could have been. The P.E.M. System is designed to enable you to organize and prioritize your daily events without being influenced by your emotions.

Once you master the P.E.M. System you'll come to the same conclusion as so many others...

There "IS" time for every important thing in my life.

Chapter 4

Slay Or Sleep With Your "Giant"

"Always do first, that which will create your future."

- TERRY GOGNA

The "Giant" is a Future-Based Event that we know we MUST perform frequently, in order to create our desired future, yet because we feel uncomfortable doing it, we constantly look for reasons to resist it at that moment in time.

We procrastinate mainly because we know there is no immediate reward for doing it now and there is no immediate painful consequence for NOT doing it now. There's no instant gratification and it won't hurt if we leave it until later.

However, every time we procrastinate, our guilt over not doing it grows and we feel even worse. This in turn decreases

"The courage we desire and prize is not the courage to die decently, but to live manfully."

- THOMAS CARLYLE

our motivation and drive to do the other things we also need to do. It's a downward spiral of despair and discouragement.

So what is the solution?

The solution is the "**MCR**" **Technique**:

1. Develop the right **Mindset**
2. Create a **Consequence**
3. Create a **Reward**

1. Always focus on slaying your Giant first, as early as possible in the day, while you are the strongest. The longer you leave it to slay your Giant, the weaker you are and the harder it will get.

Repeatedly affirm to yourself and program your mind with these words;

"I always do first, that which creates my future."

2. You must understand, deep inside your core, this absolute fact: You either choose to SLAY your Giant or you choose to SLEEP with your Giant.

It's YOUR choice.

At the beginning of each day, your Giant will jump up and climb on to your back, with his arms around your neck and his legs tightly wrapped around your waist. If you don't get him off your back as quickly as you can, you will exhaust yourself, dragging him with you every where you go.

If you don't get him off by bed time, he'll be joining you in bed. The Giant in bed represents the guilt you will feel for not doing what you know you should have done. He'll still be on your back as you get into bed. As you toss and turn he's still there, tossing and turning with you. Imagine the kind of sleep you will get with him there all night long.

Hopefully, having to sleep with your Giant is now a consequence big enough to motivate you enough to slay your Giant before you get to bed!

3. If scheduling to slay your Giant after dinner is not working for you, change it. Set the reward of, "I'll only eat after I slay my Giant." Now you have an immediate reward for slaying your Giant. Be creative and come up with your own personal "reward" solutions.

"To see what is right and not do it, is of want of courage."

- CONFUCIUS

"God is bound to act, to pour Himself into thee, as soon as He shall find thee ready."

- MEISTER ECKHART

I wish I had known about this Giant when I was at school. I always left my homework and studying for exams till the very last moment; thinking that I would always be able to cram it in.

When I was seventeen years of age, one of the subjects I was studying was "Mathematics & Statistics." I hated it with a passion so I always left it to the last minute. The day before my final exam of the year I came home from school at about 4:00pm and decided that I would stay up all night and study. I set a goal to go to bed at 6:00pm and wake up at midnight. So, like I planned, I went to bed at 6:00pm and at midnight I woke up and made my way downstairs to the kitchen where I was planning on studying. The house felt spooky and quiet like a graveyard. Everyone was sleeping quietly in their beds except me.

Before starting to study I decided to make myself some tea. I convinced myself that a cup of tea would refresh me before I started revising. Then I began to study.

I opened up a very thick binder with one year of math notes in it. I stared at the first page for about thirty seconds as though I was in a daze and then I slowly turned the page. At that very moment I began to feel a cold sweat on my face. My heart started beating a little faster and my stomach began to sink lower. My mind started spinning. I could hear fifty thousand voices in my head all shouting out mathematical equations. It was like an off-beat orchestra building up to the close. The noise was painfully loud. All of a sudden there was silence. I got up, slammed my binder shut and with total frustration and anger, threw it across the room as hard as I could. It smashed against the ground and exploded. All the papers went flying everywhere. I felt sick to my stomach. I did manage not to cry though. I just held the tears back with my frustration and discouragement. I kept asking myself, "Why did I leave it so late to revise?" "Why didn't I study earlier on in the week?"... I felt like such a loser.

For the next few minutes, I just sat paralyzed at the table. The silence was deafening. My mind was so exhausted from fighting this mental battle. I was such a procrastinator when it came to studying.

"Learn to see in another's calamity the ills, which you should avoid."

- PUBLILIUS SYRUS

35

When I finally gained my composure, I started to gather up the papers, switched off the lights and went back to bed. It was 12:45 am.

Loud knocking and shouts of, "You're going to be late for your exam," woke me up the following morning. It was my Mom. She was panicking about me missing my exam. It was an "A" Level exam, one of the most important exams of my life; the exams that determine whether or not I would qualify to go to University. My response was a shout back through the locked door of my room, "I'm not going!"

... It was not a good day.

I didn't know anything about managing events. I didn't know anything about how to slay the "Giant." I didn't know how to get myself to do what I needed to do. All I knew was that I was a compulsive procrastinator and it had finally caught up with me in a big way.

I knew I had talent, but I also knew that talent wasn't enough.

I failed miserably because I couldn't get myself to do what I needed to do. I knew that if I was ever going to amount to anything in my life, I had better learn how to solve this problem of procrastination.

"Procrastination is an invisible disease which takes a talented individual with great potential and turns him/her, slowly, bit-by-bit, over time, into a complete and utter failure."

"A foolish man is always doing, Yet much remains to be done."

- LAO TZU

Chapter 5

There Is ALWAYS Time For EVERY Important Thing In Your Life

"When one has much to put into them, a day has a hundred pockets."

- FRIEDRICH NIETZSCHE

Imagine you are in the middle of preparing for an important meeting at work and your son asks you to play "catch" with him. Would you say, "I don't have time right now?"

Imagine that you are about to leave for a meeting and your wife asks you to get some milk and bring it back home before you leave for your meeting. Would you say "I don't have time right now?"

Is this really the truth?

"It is better to allow our lives to speak for us, than our words."

- MOHANDAS GANDHI

Picture yourself at a very important meeting and you get the urge to go to the washroom. We've all been in this situation. You know you have to go immediately. What will you do? Will you say, "I don't have time?" This is proof that **we each have the time to do whatever we want to, as long as it is important enough to us.**

Never say you "don't have time." Instead, tell yourself the truth; "It is not an important enough event at this time, to justify allocating any of my time to it now." In other words, you don't consider it to be a priority event at this moment in time.

Imagine it's 8:00pm on a Monday night and Mary is about to make some prospecting calls for her business. All of a sudden her seven-year-old daughter asks her to play with her. Mary doesn't want her daughter to get upset and she wants to be a good mother, so she drops everything and decides to play.

Once the playing is done, Mary realizes that it's 9:30pm and it's now too late to make any calls for her business, so she decides to put off making the calls until tomorrow.

It is now Tuesday 8:00pm and Mary is about to make some prospecting calls for her business. The phone rings and she sees on the "call display" that it is a friend calling. Instead of letting the answering machine handle the call, she convinces herself that it may be important and answers it. When Mary finally hangs up the phone, she realizes that it's 9:30pm and it's again too late to make any calls for her business. She says to herself "I'll make twice as many calls tomorrow."   ...What is happening here?

Mary does not realize that she has relinquished control of the events in her life; interruptions, distractions and Mary's emotions are in control of the events in her life.

Mary, like a sail boat without a rudder, is being directed by the wind. When the wind blows from the east, the boat (Mary) moves westbound. When the wind blows from the west the boat (Mary) moves eastbound. But one day in the near future, when the wind finally stops blowing for a moment, Mary will sadly realize she is nowhere near where she actually wanted to be in her life at the age she's at.

"Failure is the path of least resistance."

- SIR JAMES MATTHEW BARRIE

"There is always time for every important thing in your life."

- TERRY GOGNA

The only question is whether she will know why she isn't where she wanted to be or whether she will simply say in her sorrow, "How can this be; I work so hard, I'm always so busy, why am I not further ahead in my life?"

This is why the "Priority Event Management System" is so important to our success in life: **It prioritizes and then organizes the events in our lives in such a way that we always have time to do the things we SHOULD be doing.**

We don't have to say, "I don't have time" and we don't have to let unexpected interruptions take over our lives.

Mirror, Mirror, On The Wall, Will I Finish This Paperwork, Before I Fall?

Have you ever said this to yourself?

"Let me just get this paperwork out of the way and then my mind will be freed up so I can focus on my real work."

Don't get sucked into this BIG LIE.

Paperwork never ends; it just changes its face. Like a multi-headed monster, just when you think you have won by cutting its head off, another head grows in its place.

Paperwork is like TIME; it always exists, whether you do or not.

So what's the solution?

Don't waste your time doing paperwork EVERYDAY. Only do that which has to be done today. Otherwise you'll fall into the trap of trying to complete something that has no end.

"Our knowledge is the amassed thought and experience of innumerable minds."

- RALPH WALDO EMERSON

43

> *"I am always doing that which I cannot do in order that I may learn how to do it."*
>
> - PABLO PICASSO

Once a week, set aside a specific amount of time to complete the paperwork that you have accumulated for the week. Usually, twenty to thirty minutes will be ample time to dissolve most piles of paperwork.

A Solution For Scattered Paperwork:

1. Get an "accordion-type" folder with compartments.

2. Number each compartment from one to thirty-one, for the days of the month.

3. Put in it, ONLY the paperwork that has a specific deadline date on it. Put the paperwork in the appropriate day's compartment. Now, you won't have to shuffle paperwork until the day you need to do it.

4. Get a box or office tray and put in it all the remaining paperwork without a deadline date on it, plus all paperwork that you want to complete on your next specific weekly paperwork day. Now you have freed up more time to spend on important things rather than shuffling the SAME paperwork everyday.

"Honey, Can You Fix The ...?"

Have you ever heard a man say, "My wife keeps bugging me about chores that need to be done around the house and I keep putting them off"?

The real reason most men put off jobs around the house is because they feel it will take up too much of their "valuable" relaxation/fun time on the weekend. And, they can actually live without finishing "the thing" that needs to be finished; it doesn't really bother them that much to see it unfinished.

However, fellow men, we need to understand that every time our wives see that unfinished job in the house, it drains her energy. Ultimately, we will feel the consequences of this "drained energy" in other areas of our relationship.

...If you know what I mean guys!

It is very important to understand that most wives want to feel good about their home. It's a "pride of ownership" thing.

"First learn the meaning of what you say, and then speak."

- EPICTETUS

45

> *"When anger rises, think of the consequences."*
>
> - Confucius

The home environment completes them and gives them joy & inner peace, as long as everything is finished.

Solution For Men:
Set aside some time very early in the day e.g. 8:00am Saturday morning, when you normally sleep-in. If you do it early enough, it will seem as though you haven't used any part of your regular Saturday to do it in.

Solution For Ladies:
Asking someone to do something repeatedly is "nagging." Stop nagging your husband EVERY weekend. It's not good for either of you; simply get a date and time from him and WRITE IT DOWN in his P.E.M. System Planner. That's it, it's done!

Chapter 6

You Are In A War And The Battleground Is Inside Your Head

> *"Men are not prisoners of fate, but only prisoners of their own minds."*
>
> - FRANKLIN D. ROOSEVELT

The seeds of our future are the Future-Based events that we must carry out each day. If we don't plant the seeds on a daily basis we will have nothing to look forward to in the future.

We must adopt the mindset that we are in a "mental war." Every day is a battle against the random forces that are focused on killing our seeds. The question we need to ask each day is, "Who is going to win today's battle?"

What are the forces that will try to kill the seeds of our future?

"What we obtain too cheaply, we esteem too lightly."

- THOMAS PAINE

First, understand that these forces are not in unison; they are not acting together as one force. They are individual random forces that have no order, but can destroy our future if we are not prepared for each of their attacks.

Before we can win the war (achieve our desired future), we must win the daily battles and understand the weapons that will be used against us:

- Distractions
- Interruptions
- Mood swings
- Set backs

Once you plan your day by inputting your Future-Based and Present-Based events into your P.E.M. System, be ready to **"defend your ground."** Make sure you are aware of the different kinds of enemies that could attack you at anytime of the day and get you off track.

Get a piece of paper right now and make a list of possible attacks to be prepared for.

Here are some suggestions to consider:

Possible Attacks/Distractions:

1. Incoming calls
2. E-mail
3. Internet surfing
4. MSN messenger
5. Paperwork
6. "Let me just clean up a little first"
7. Television
8. An urge to take a break for a snack
9. "I'm not in the mood"
10. An urge to "start fresh tomorrow" by dropping everything & rescheduling all your daily events to tomorrow
11. "It's getting late; I should go to bed because I'm getting up early tomorrow and I don't want to be tired at work"
12. "I think I'll sleep in a little longer, I can always catch up later"
13. Someone's request for you to do something
14. Unexpected guest
15. Legitimate emergency

"True success is being at peace with the stress."

- TERRY GOGNA

Now prepare a list of counter-attacks to each possible attack/distraction. Here are some suggestions:

Counter-Attacks And Ways To Avoid Being Attacked/Distracted:

1. Incoming calls

Whenever the phone rings, especially during a Future-Based event, do not answer it personally; let the answering machine handle it. Once the message comes in, check it and answer it ONLY when you have to.

2. E-mails

Remove the temptation completely by turning off your computer, at least until your Future-Based event is completed.

3. Internet surfing

Remove the temptation completely by turning off your computer, at least until your Future-Based event is completed.

4. MSN messenger

Remove the temptation completely by turning off your computer, at least until your Future-Based event is completed.

5. Paperwork

Set aside time to do your paperwork as an event, so it doesn't interrupt other events.

6. "Let me just clean up a little first"
If you can't do it in thirty seconds leave it alone.

7. Television
Set a time for TV watching as an event, don't let it be a temptation.

8. An urge to take a break for a snack
Schedule your breaks into your P.E.M. System ahead of time, then follow your plan and don't give in to your emotions to change it on the day.

9. "I don't feel in the mood"
Don't give in, ignore it. It'll only last a minute or so. You'll be glad you fought it and won.

10. An urge to "start fresh tomorrow" by dropping everything and changing all of your daily events to tomorrow
Fight it with everything you've got. This is procrastination at its worst. It is totally unnecessary to do this. Starting again tomorrow doesn't suddenly make things easier, especially knowing that you gave up the day before. This is now a test of "stamina and resolve."

"The unexamined life is not worth living."

- SOCRATES

"To be worn out is to be renewed."

- LAO-TZU

You need to stick to your original game plan and prove to yourself that you have the tenacity to do what you said you would do and not give up.

11. "It's getting late; I should go to bed because I'm getting up early tomorrow and I don't want to be tired at work"

It's a lie, stop listening to yourself. If you were going to Hawaii tomorrow you wouldn't care about the lack of sleep. Stick to the program and follow your planned events in your P.E.M. System.

12. "I think I'll sleep in a little longer, I can always catch up later"

Do something, do anything, just get out of that bed before you fall into the next "deep-sleep-cycle." It's a trap. Fight the temptation to sleep-in with everything you've got. Once you get yourself out of bed, wash your face immediately. In ten seconds or less, you'll feel perfectly fine and realize that your "body" was lying to you; you didn't need anymore sleep.

13. Someone's request for you to do something

Look in your planner and give the person a date and a time when you can carry out their request.

14. Unexpected guest

Ask someone else to answer the door for you.

15. Legitimate Emergency

How good are you at *recovery*; getting back on track when you are forced to get off track? How fast can you set in action, "Game Plan B?" Until you get good at *recovery* you will have to "take-the-hit" and suffer the consequences, whatever they may be.

I would recommend putting this list of possible attacks/distractions up on your office wall. Pay very close attention to them, especially when you are carrying out your Future-Based Events.

"Nothing gives one person so much advantage over another, as to remain always cool and unruffled under all circumstances."

- THOMAS JEFFERSON

Chapter 7

Self Discovery

"A thinker sees his own actions as experiments; as attempts to find out something. Success and failure are for him answers above all."

- FRIEDRICH NIETZSCHE

The P.E.M. System, as well as being a priority organizer and planner, is also a self discovery tool that will enable you to learn a tremendous amount about yourself and your working habits.

For example, let's say you decide you want to seriously take up exercising. So you plan to get up every morning at 6:00am before work to exercise for an hour. After two days, you give up exercising because it just isn't working; you can't get yourself out of bed at 6:00am, so you say to yourself, "Exercising is just not for me. I guess I'll never be fit."

"He who knows others is wise; He who knows himself is enlightened."

- LAO-TZU

Six months later you're watching TV late at night and you see a program about the benefits of an exercise program. You get all fired up and decide to take up exercising again.

You convince yourself that this time it will be different because you are not going to schedule it in for the early morning but instead you are going to exercise as your last event of the day, just before bed.

Two days later you quit again because you are too tired to exercise before bed. So once more, you say to yourself, "This 'exercising thing' is just not for me. I guess I'll have to forget about being fit."

What's the solution here?

The solution is in the **P.E.M. System.** It is simple, but not obvious.

It's not that this person doesn't like exercising or doesn't want to be fit. The fact is they cannot maintain an exercise routine at 6:00am or at night just before bed; these are the facts, nothing else.

If a person normally struggles to get up at 6:00am and now they decide to get up at 6:00am AND exercise, they are seriously asking for trouble; now they have to deal with two things they don't like.

"The worst loneliness is not to be comfortable with yourself."

- MARK TWAIN

The simplest solution is to change the time of the exercise routine as many times as it takes, until they DISCOVER the best time to do it at.

The best time to exercise is hidden somewhere in the P.E.M. System, waiting to be discovered. It could be at lunch time, right after work at 5:00pm or even somewhere in the middle of the evening.

Each individual needs to use the P.E.M. System as a self discovery tool and rearrange whatever events that they need to rearrange until all "planned" Future-Based and Present-Based events are completed on a regular basis.

The focus should NOT be on giving up on an event if it's not being done, but to adjust the time of the event UNTIL it gets done.

Chapter 8

It's All About The "Results"

> *"You will bring results in accordance with the breadth of your mindset."*
>
> - Rev Sun Myung Moon

If you give a job to someone with a deadline of one hour to complete it when it can really be done in forty minutes, most people will take the full hour to finish the job because that's what was given to them.

There's a phrase we have all heard at one time or another...

"If you want something done, ask a busy person."

Like parrots, people repeat this phrase over and over, yet never take a moment to see how inaccurate it is.

"Your results are your only true proof of your efforts."

- Terry Gogna

Even though most successful people are busy people, there are far more "busy unsuccessful" people in the world. The primary reason for their failure is that they are busy doing all the wrong things. Busy putting out fires. Busy attending to their present life, yet too busy to make time to do the things that will create a new and better future for themselves.

If you want something done, ask somebody who's good at getting things done.

Your results are your only true credibility.

The overall goal within each day should be to **get more done in less time**.

To increase your results there are two questions you should always ask yourself at the end of each day:

1. How could I have done more in the time I had?

2. How could I have been more effective and gotten better results, in the time I had?

How Can I Do More In The Time I Have?

Two suggestions:

1. Push Yourself Harder

Just as in physical training workouts where you strive to beat your previous best, do the same with stretching yourself when it comes to daily events. Push yourself to wake up fifteen minutes earlier on certain days, push yourself to go to bed fifteen minutes later and push yourself to complete tasks faster than you would normally.

You don't have to do it all the time but at least do it some of the time so you can increase your daily "stamina" of effectiveness and productivity.

A wise person was once asked, "How long do you really want to live?" His reply was, "As long as I am healthy, I would like to live to about one hundred and twenty years of age; I have a lot of things I want to accomplish on this earth before I have to leave it."

"The heights by great men reached and kept, were not attained by sudden flight, but they while their companions slept, were toiling upward in the night."

- HENRY WADSWORTH LONGFELLOW

If you knew the exact day and time that you would be leaving this earth, how precious would each day and hour be to you, knowing that every day, and every hour that passes is gone forever and pushes you closer to that very day?

The only question left to ask is, **What did you actually do with the day or hour that just passed?**

Imagine if you had to earn your time on earth. Imagine that depending on how you spent the hours of each day, how productive & effective you are with your time and how the events that you carry out, benefit not only yourself, but others; imagine if these were the things that actually determined whether or not you got to live another day.

How would you live now?

Imagine if God asked you this question:

"Why should I give you another year or month or week or even another day of life on this earth; what do you plan on doing with it?"

2. Multi-Task Whenever Possible

Multi-tasking is an excellent skill to acquire. It will enable you to get more done in less time. Always search for ways you can multi-task. When you do, you'll be amazed at how much more time you will open up for yourself.

As you input your events into the P.E.M. System always ask yourself how you can multi-task two events at the same time.

Here are some suggestions:

Listen to educational CDs:
- While showering, driving or eating

Check voice-mail:
- While eating or "waiting"

Check e-mails:
-While eating or between phone calls

Read:
- While "waiting" or between phone calls

"Your results, are your only true credibility."

- TERRY GOGNA

"I have not failed. I've just found 10,000 ways that won't work."

- THOMAS EDISON

With practice & focus you'll be amazed at how good you will get at multi-tasking and how much more you will be able to accomplish in a day.

I've always loved this powerful statement by Mike Murdock:

"Men fail because of broken focus."

However, from my personal experience, today I would tend to lean more towards this realization:

There is no such thing as broken focus. People always have perfect focus on something. However, people fail because they choose to focus and spend time on the wrong things; things that WILL NOT create their desired future.

Chapter 9

The "Layout" Of Your Day

The layout of your day will influence greatly what you accomplish in a day.

There are two very important features to pay attention to when choosing a daily planner:

1. The actual "size of the space" that is designated for each day.

2. The "time of day" written on each of the lines throughout the day.

How many events can you fit into a two-inch box designated as one of your days of the week?

The smaller the space designated for each day, the less you will get done. It is not wise to use this kind of a tool for planning your day if you want to be productive. However, it is good to carry with you when you are on the move; to look up a date and use it as a "temporary notebook planner," with the intention of transferring the information to your main planner when you get home.

Most planners found in stationary stores have the "times of the day" written like this:

```
8  _____
9  _____
10 _____
11 _____
12 _____
1  _____
2  _____
3  _____
4  _____
5  _____
6  _____
7  _____
```

Sometimes you will also see the "times of the day" in thirty minute segments.

Here's what's wrong with the layout of these planners:

1. They are designed primarily for your daytime profession and not for your personal life in the evening.

2. You are not able to organize any events before 8:00am or after 7:00pm with this particular planner layout.

3. If you write an event on the 3:00pm line which only take ten minutes to accomplish; what happens to the time between 3:10pm and 4:00pm? There is no room to write an event that you want to do at 3:10pm. This type of poor planning will cost you a lot of wasted time throughout your whole day.

4. It is very difficult to plan multi-tasking with this layout.

5. You will not be able to measure and see at a glance the **unused-time** in your day with this kind of layout.

The "unused-time" is like "hidden treasure" in your day. It must first be found before it has value.

"Dost thou love life? Then do not squander time, for that's the stuff life is made of."

- BENJAMIN FRANKLIN

71

"Learn to labor and to wait."

- HENRY WADSWORTH LONGFELLOW

The Floater

There will be times that you have a particular event that you must do sometime throughout the course of the day but you don't know when, so you cannot write it down as a specific event in your P.E.M. System. When this situation arises, write the event on a small sticky paper and stick the paper onto your "P.E.M. System Daily Template," close to the time when you feel you may be able to do it. The sticky paper is referred to as "The Floater." As the day progresses move the floater to the next possible time where you think you might be able to carry out this event. If it is still not done at that time, keep moving it forward until it eventually gets done.

The "One-Planner" Principle

A person with two watches on their wrist never really knows what the correct time is.

You should only use ONE planner to organize your personal & professional life.

The only exception would be if you are forced to use a planner at work, strictly for your job. In this case you would have two planners; one that stays at work for your job and one that you use for your personal life, after work hours.

Your fridge calendar should not be used as your personal and professional event planner. It is a "notice board." Take the things written on it and input them into your P.E.M. System Planner.

In conclusion:

People plan their workday professionally because they want to achieve success in their profession.

"In order to achieve a significant level of success in your personal life, you must plan your personal life, professionally."

"It is no use saying, 'we are doing our best.' You have got to succeed in doing what is necessary."

- WINSTON CHURCHILL

Chapter 10

"P.E.M. System Tips" For Sales Professionals

"All speech is vain and empty unless it be accompanied by action."

- Demosthenes

In most companies, prospecting calls are the main method for generating new business and consistent neglect in this area will always lead to eventual business failure.

Making prospecting calls is the single most important event in a professional salesperson's day.

If your goal is to make prospecting calls for one hour, to be productive you must have an exact number of calls that you are aiming to accomplish within that hour.

"It does not matter how slowly you go, as long as you do not stop."

- CONFUCIUS

Let's assume you are shooting to make twelve calls within one hour.

First

Specify the exact hour you are going to make the calls, let's say 7:00pm.

Second

Write the number of calls (12) that you are shooting to accomplish within that hour directly on the "P.E.M. System Daily Template" as you see in the diagram below:

7:00	1		
	2		
	3		
7:15	4		
	5		
	6		
7:30	7		
	8		
	9		
7:45	10		
	11		
	12		

The purpose of this layout is to get you to race against time. You have five minutes for each call. There is no time for procrastinating or celebrating; keep moving and keep an eye on the time.

If you feel you can do more than twelve calls within one hour, you may prefer this layout:

7:00	1	
	2	
	3	4
7:15	5	
	6	
	7	8
7:30	9	
	10	
	11	12
7:45	13	
	14	
	15	16

Remember to always write your target calls on the P.E.M. System Daily Template (as shown above) **before** the day of the calls; specify when and how many calls you want to make.

Keep a record of your BEST HOUR and your BEST DAY.

"Never fear the want of business. A man who qualifies himself well for his calling, never fails of employment."

- THOMAS JEFFERSON

"Not to know what has been transacted in the former times is to be always a child. If no use is made of the labors of past ages, the world must remain always in the infancy of knowledge."

- CICERO

Your BEST HOUR is the highest number of prospecting calls you made in one hour.

Your BEST DAY is the highest number of prospecting calls you made in one day, regardless of when you made the calls.

Just like in physical fitness, the goal of the workout is to beat your previous best. So every time you make calls, **have a goal to beat your BEST HOUR and your BEST DAY.**

This mindset will focus you on being more effective and productive every time you make calls.

Always remember, you can't beat your best unless you know what your best is, so always **"know your number"** and keep it in front of you when you make your calls.

What Did You Learn?

When you set a goal and hit it, very rarely do you ever learn anything.

It's when you miss or pass your goal that you have an opportunity to learn new things.

So don't be discouraged when you miss the goals you set. Just understand that you still need to learn certain necessary things in order to achieve the success you are looking to achieve.

As long as you are persistently applying consistent effort, it's only a matter of time until all the necessary lessons are learned and you arrive at your desired future.

Let's say you set a goal for the week to make twelve prospecting calls every day. At the end of the week you review your results and they look like this:

	Goal	Achieved
M	12	12
T	12	6
W	12	20
T	12	12
F	12	12

"Let me tell you the secret that has led me to my goal. My strength lies solely in my tenacity."

- LOUIS PASTEUR

"From error to error, one discovers entire truth."

- SIGMUND FREUD

From the weekly review it's obvious that something happened on Tuesday because only six calls were made. This is an ideal opportunity to learn a very valuable lesson.

On a separate piece of paper write down what got in your way. What exactly stopped you from hitting your goal?

Whatever you do, do not misplace this list. Every time you miss your goal write down the exact thing that caused you to miss your goal, no matter what it was: people, feelings or situations. It doesn't matter, write it down.

After a couple of weeks, upon reviewing this list, you'll notice something very strange. The list of things that stop you from hitting your goal will actually be quite small because the same things keep coming up.

You want to get to the point where everything is listed and there's nothing new each week. The point of this exercise is to show you that these are the only things that are in your way to achieving your desired future. Once you handle these, you win; you made it.   … Mission accomplished!

What Do I Do With The List?

As soon as you have one obstacle on your list, you need to set a game plan of attack:

1. What can you do to prevent this obstacle from coming up again?

2. If you cannot prevent it, what is the best way to handle it, so it doesn't stop you from hitting your goal?

I Passed My Goal... Now What?

Referring back to the weekly review, it is also obvious that something great happened on Wednesday - twenty calls were made instead of twelve. This is again an ideal opportunity to learn a very valuable lesson. If we can do twenty calls once, we can do it again. The question is, what did we do differently that caused us to exceed the goal we set? Once we know this, all we have to do is repeat it.

"It's not that I'm so smart, it's just that I stay with problems longer."

- ALBERT EINSTEIN

I'm Not Consistent With My Calls; I Only Make Them When I Feel Good

Professionals act regardless of how they feel. If you want the results of a professional you must figure out a way to temporarily ignore your "mood of the moment." In these situations your feelings/thoughts are *lying* to you. Ignore them and make the calls anyway.

Two techniques that will help:

1. "Click and Pick"

Before you pick up the phone to make a call, click/snap your fingers first and then pick up the phone. Do this EVERYTIME you make a call no matter how strange it feels.

After a week or two of conditioning yourself this way, you'll be amazed that no matter how you feel, as soon as you click your fingers you automatically reach for the phone and are ready to dial. **You have successfully conditioned yourself to overcome the power of your mood/feelings simply with a click of your fingers.**

2. Only The First Call Is Your "Road-Block" To Success

If you don't have the correct mindset before you start your calls, you may never make them. You must have the correct picture in your head of the first call that you are about to make.

The amateur believes that each and every call will be just as emotionally draining as the first call. This is NOT true.

"Many of life's failures are people who did not realize how close they were to success when they gave up."

- THOMAS EDISON

The Amateur's Mindset:

Every call?

"A hero is no braver than an ordinary man, but he is braver five minutes longer."

- RALPH WALDO EMERSON

The professional knows that the first call is the ONLY "road-block" to success. This is absolutely TRUE.

The Professional's Mindset:

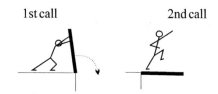

1st call   2nd call

I Hit All My Goals...Now What?

If your goal was to make twelve calls every day and you accomplished it, then you need to take the next step:

You need to understand that your goal is too small and because you are hitting it every time, you are no longer stretching yourself mentally. As a result, you are also no longer growing.

In life we are either growing or dying, there is no middle ground.

Your next step should be to raise your goal to maybe fifteen calls each day. By doing this, you will then create again for yourself further opportunity for more growth.

Repeat this process over and over again until you achieve your desired future.

"Life grants nothing to us mortals, without hard work."

- HORACE

Chapter 11

Create Your Own Personal "Success Environment"

> *"The most onerous slavery is to be a slave to oneself."*
>
> - SENECA

Have you ever had any of these thoughts?

- I can't believe I did that again!
- Why did I lose my temper so easily?
- I can't believe that I said that!
- Why am I so afraid?
- Why can't I be more patient?
- Why is my willpower so weak?
- Why was I so rude to that person?
- How did I get on this road?
- Why can't I be more affectionate?
- Why am I always so selfish?
- Why can't I decide faster?
- I don't want to be like this.
- Why do I always worry so much?
- Why can't I get myself to do this?
- What is wrong with me?

Nothing is wrong with any of us; we are all "Perfect Products" of our environment.

Our environment has perfectly programmed us to think and behave the way we do, through the things we have personally seen, heard, smelled, tasted and touched within it.

Our programming has come from two distinct environments:

1. As a child, we were programmed by the environment that we are brought up in. This environment, whether good or bad, was enforced upon us, we had no choice.

2. **As an adult we further program ourselves, by the environment that we consistently CHOOSE to expose ourselves to.**

Before we sit down to eat a meal, do we have to actively think about the process of how to feed ourselves? Imagine saying this to yourself every time you are about to eat: "I have to hold my spoon like this. Now I have to lower it to the bowl of cereal. Now I have to scoop up the cereal into my spoon and slowly and carefully bring it up to my mouth. Now I have to open my mouth and direct the spoon into my mouth and then close my mouth."

Of course we don't do this. We can put the food automatically into our mouths without even thinking about it.

However, this was exactly what we did as a child when we first tried eating with a spoon. By repeating this action over and over again it eventually became second-nature; an automatic response.

Our subconscious mind wants to make our lives easier. It looks for actions that we do repeatedly and records them as automatic responses. After a certain number of repetitions, whatever that number may be, there will come a time that as soon as we start to act in a certain way, our subconscious mind will then automatically assume that it knows what we want to accomplish and take over. **It will finish the event for us, without us even being actively aware of it.**

Eating, drinking, riding a bike, walking, driving, talking, swimming & writing, are just a few examples of automatic responses.

"The beginning is the most important part of the work."

- PLATO

89

"We are, what we repeatedly do."

- ARISTOTLE

The subconscious mind does not only store our physical actions, it stores anything & everything we experience through our five senses.

For example, if we repeatedly lose our temper in certain situations and actually get what we want, even though our behaviour is poor, our subconscious mind will record it as an event. Then every time we are in the early stages of a similar situation in the future, our subconscious will take over and we will automatically lose our temper again in order to get what we want. Our bad behaviour is being rewarded and recorded as a successful way to get what we want, even though it is the wrong way to get it.

Here's another example: We throw garbage into a garbage bin that is in a specific place in our office, repeatedly over many days. If we move the garbage bin we will still, without realizing at first, throw the garbage onto the floor where the bin used to be.

When bringing up stored information from the past, our subconscious mind always brings up first, those experiences that have strong emotions attached to them and secondly, those actions that we have constantly repeated over and over again in the past.

If we've ever had reason to be afraid of something that has happened to us in the past, when a similar situation arises in the future, in order to protect us, our subconscious mind will first bring up our most emotional past experience of the fear and secondly the most repeated experience. It is reminding us that we were previously afraid of this experience and we should again be on our guard.

However, most people are not exactly empowered by these reminders of their past experiences, especially if they are not positive reminders. Instead of being on guard, most people become discouraged and as a result, do not move on with their lives. Reminders of past failures, past rejections and past bad feelings don't exactly motivate us to do more.

Even though it exists to protect us and make our lives easier, most of the time our subconscious mind actually works

"We do not keep the outward form of order, where there is deep disorder in the mind."

- WILLIAM SHAKESPEARE

91

"If one speaks or acts with a cruel mind, misery follows, as the cart follows the horse... If one speaks or acts with a pure mind, happiness follows, as a shadow follows its source."

- THE DHAMMAPADA

against us in building a better life because of the poor content we have put into it over the previous years.

The life & the quality of relationships we have today are a direct result of our behaviour.

Our behaviour is a direct result of our beliefs.

Our beliefs are actually reminders of "the results of our past experiences," embedded deep in our subconscious mind.

Therefore, the content of our subconscious mind will make or break our future.

The key to our future lies in the ability to somehow alter the content of our subconscious mind in our favour.

How Do We "Actively" Change The Content Of Our Subconscious Mind?

We cannot erase or remove or de-program the existing content of our subconscious mind. We can only add content to it that may eventually overpower the existing content in our favour.

Example:

If you put a drop of blue ink into a glass of water, the water will turn blue. If you then pour the glass of blue water into a swimming pool of clear water, it will be impossible for you to see the ink. You have diluted the ink to the point where it is now absolutely powerless. Yet remember, you have not removed the ink - it is still in the water. This is exactly what you must do to the content of your subconscious mind; dilute the "negative" content to the degree that it becomes powerless and can no longer stop you from achieving your desired future.

"Except our own thoughts, there is nothing absolutely in our power."

- RENE DESCARTES

"Once a word has been allowed to escape, it cannot be recalled."

- HORACE

You must flood your subconscious mind with **empowering, emotional and repetitive content**, to the degree that when it brings up beliefs/reminders of your past experiences, those reminders actually empower you to act and succeed.

How Do You Actively Input Content Into Your Subconscious Mind?

Imagine if you could actually look into your subconscious mind and take inventory of everything that was in there. Imagine if this was the kind of information you discovered:

- 850 Experiences of "rejection"
- 625 Experiences of "acceptance"

Therefore, **225 experiences of "rejection" are currently in power.**

- 450 Experiences of "losing temper and getting what you wanted"
- 232 Experiences of "losing temper and not getting what you wanted"

Therefore, **218 experiences of "losing temper and getting what you wanted" are currently in power.**

- 1100 "Failures after attempts"
- 343 "Successes after attempts"
Therefore **757 experiences of "failures after attempts" are currently in power.**

Wouldn't having this kind of information be absolutely empowering to you in your life?

It is well known that the subconscious mind does not know the difference between reality and imagination. With focus and a lot of practice, you can actually use your imagination to create powerful positive imaginary situations. Then one at a time, input them into your subconscious mind by making yourself experience each of these situations through the power of your imagination.

The content that we "actively" put into our subconscious mind is referred to as an **"affirmation statement."**

Affirmation statements are always written in **"positive-present-tense"** language.

"Cogito ergo sum... I think; therefore I am."

- RENE DESCARTES

95

"There is nothing good or bad, but thinking makes it so."

- WILLIAM SHAKESPEARE

Not only can we program our subconscious mind with affirmations to empower our behaviour, but it is a known fact that we can use the power of affirmations, as long as they are accompanied by strong emotions, to actually attract the things we want in our lives: opportunities, people, money, etc. Whatever we want we can attract into our lives.

At the end of this chapter I have listed many examples of affirmations. I would strongly recommend that you review the list carefully and then create your own. Make sure you write each affirmation individually on separate cards; 3"x5" file cards or even the back of business cards work great.

Do not write all of your affirmations on one piece of paper because you will be constantly re-writing many of them as you progress through this exercise.

Once you have written out your affirmations, the next thing to do is to set a time each day to **read, out loud**, each affirmation at least five times. It is very important to read them out at **least five times** because by the third time, our ears will actually clue into what we are reading. By the fourth time we will start paying full attention and on the fifth time, the message will actively sink into our subconscious mind.

"Where the speech is corrupted, the mind is also."

- SENECA

As you read your affirmations, be as passionate as you can; capture and internalize the emotion of what you are saying. At the same time, use the power of your imagination and visualize what you want. See yourself experiencing exactly that which you are saying.

By the way, cutting out and pasting pictures onto your affirmation cards will help create a more powerful visual experience.

Putting up affirmations on your office wall, on your car dashboard, on your bathroom wall or even on your fridge are excellent ways to create your own personal "success environment."

You must also accept the fact that this process will take practice and focus, so give yourself time.

"Prayer indeed is good, but while calling on the gods, a man should himself lend a hand."

- Hippocrates

If you have "757 experiences of failure" already embedded in your subconscious mind, you will need to input your affirmation statements 757 times just to equalize what is already in your subconscious mind. So don't give up after a week if you don't see any results. It may take a month, 6 months, or even a year for you to change some automatic behaviours and beliefs.

Keep in mind, your subconscious mind is not going to stop recording and storing experiences just because you have started saying affirmations. It is still going to keep doing what it is designed to do.

By the way, don't make the mistake of thinking that you will be able to change your whole world by ONLY doing affirmations. Remember, you're doing this affirmation exercise to empower yourself to have positive/winning thoughts/beliefs/reminders; **you still have to act. You still have to do something to create your future.** The affirmation exercise alone will not create your desired future; it's main purpose is **to shut up the "little voice in your head" long enough so you can do what you need to do, to win.**

In the Book of Genesis, in the Old Testament, it says that God **spoke** the world into existence; perhaps this is a clue that we should at least try this exercise for ourselves.

The exercise of creating and repeating affirmations is actually a process of creating your own unique and personal success environment. Remember, you are a "Perfect Product" of your environment.

Before I say my daily affirmations, I always like to read these special words first to get myself into the right frame of mind: "God is my Heavenly Father. He made me in his image. God created the world by speaking it into existence. I, His Son, am empowered and encouraged by my Heavenly Father to also speak and create my own future into existence. Let all who can hear: the people of the physical world, the saints, the angels and the good spirits of the spirit world, the future I desire, the future I expect, the future I speak and confess with my words is the future that I, together with my Heavenly Father, will create for my family and myself. And to all the angels, if you are waiting for my request, I am asking you for your help. I am requesting

"I have never been hurt by anything I didn't say."

- CALVIN COOLIDGE

99

your help. I am expecting your help. I am thanking you for your help. Hear my words, in the name of my Heavenly Father, I desire, I claim, I declare and I expect my affirmations to absolutely come true.

Here are some examples of affirmations:

Physical Health
- My body is in perfect health
- I am 150 lbs of lean muscle
- I am at 10% body fat
- I run 3km in 12mins

Mental Health
- My affirmations always come true
- I have an excellent memory. I always recall things immediately when I need them
- My mind is in perfect health
- I only hear positive and Godly thoughts in my mind
- I always make the right decision quickly if I need to
- A miracle is going to happen in my life today
- I always focus on what needs to be done and I do it
- I always do whatever it takes

- I'm going to make a brilliant discovery today
- My today and my future will be better than anything in the past
- I always enjoy the journey
- I live life to the fullest each and every day

My Character
- I'm a great listener
- I'm very patient
- I have so much charisma and energy; people are attracted to me like a magnet
- I always act immediately to help anyone in need
- My language is always clean, Godly and respectful
- I'm always caring
- I'm truly happy and grateful for all the blessings in my life
- Every time I get rejected, I get even more determined to succeed
- I always finish what I start
- I already have the confidence I need to accomplish my goals

"While thou livest, keep a good tongue in thy head."

- WILLIAM SHAKESPEARE

> *"A slip of the foot may soon recover, but a slip of the tongue you may never get over."*
>
> - BENJAMIN FRANKLIN

Relationships

- I always say and do things that make my spouse/partner feel special
- I always listen to my spouse/partner without judgment or advice
- My spouse/partner and I are best friends; we're always talking and doing fun stuff together
- I always hug my kids
- I always listen "quickly" and talk to my kids with respect
- I always tell my kids I'm proud of them and I trust them
- I have a great relationship with my kids because I always "join them in their world"
- I never embarrass my kids in front of others to make a point
- I'm always there for my brothers & sisters
- I always talk to my parents with respect

Spiritual

- I always ask God for advice before I do anything major
- I'm aware of God's heart at all times; I always do the right thing
- I'm a true representative of _____ (*name of hero, mentor, spiritual leader*) through my thoughts, words and my actions
- I have a very deep and close relationship with my heavenly father; we are always talking
- Father, thank you for teaching me how to do in 2 years what would normally take 20

Financial

- Money keeps coming to me easily from so many places
- My business is growing like crazy
- I'm the number one performer at my job
- It's the year 2010; I'm mortgage free
- It's the year 2008; my income is $_____/month
- I have $_____ cash in the bank

> *"Speak clearly, if you speak at all; carve every word before you let it fall."*
>
> - OLIVER WENDELL HOLMES

> *"It is easier to exclude harmful passions than to rule them, and to deny them admittance than to control them after they have been admitted."*
>
> - SENECA

Dreams
- I own a fully loaded Hummer and a BMW convertible (*add pictures*)
- I own a beautiful waterfront home
- I go on a family cruise every year
- I am a very successful _____ (*profession*)
- I am excellent at _____ (*hobby*)

There are many more examples of affirmations that could be listed here; I'm sure you now have enough ideas to create your own personal list.

Another group of affirmations I would like to discuss here are affirmations that counter-attack the negative power of worries.

Worries are simply NEGATIVE affirmations.

Some people worry so much that they have absolutely no motivation left to get up and do something to better their lives.

When we worry about something, we actually play out that worry in our minds, over and over again. We are creating repetitive, emotional and negative experiences that haven't even happened yet and inputting them into our subconscious mind.

By worrying, we are actually affirming and empowering the worries to manifest themselves into our lives.

Here's a solution:

1. Never leave worries in your head for too long. They will spin around and around, leaving no room for you to think about anything else. Take them out of your head and write them down on a card. As you do this you'll be amazed at how your feelings change almost immediately.

2. Now ask yourself, "Do I have any other things that I'm worried about?" If there are more, write them on another card. Keep asking yourself the same question until you finally hear yourself saying, "No, that's it; I have no other worries."

3. On the back of each "worry-card" re-write the worry in a positive affirmation statement.

"Everything you can imagine is real."

- PABLO PICASSO

4. Add these to your daily affirmation statements, but say them first.

Repeat this exercise every time you find yourself constantly worrying about something.

By the way, repetitive thoughts are just as powerful and also just as dangerous as repetitive words. Even though the people around you cannot hear your thoughts, you and your subconscious mind can.

In order to counter-act a negative thought, simply speak the same thought in a positive way immediately upon hearing the thought. You do not have to speak the words out-loud. Whispering them to yourself will drown out the negative thought instantly. Keep saying the positive words until you feel confident that the thought is gone ... at least for now.

An "affirmation" in this context is a repeated thought or spoken word, wrapped in strong emotion.

The greater the emotion behind your repetitive thoughts/words, the more likely they will manifest into your life.

Most people do not realize that there have been many events in their past that were actually true examples and proof of the power of affirmations.

Look back carefully into your own life and you will see evidence of these special "happenings." Look for things that you were emotionally wrapped up in, and that you constantly thought about, that eventually came true.

Here are three examples of affirmations that have played-out in my life:

1. Sometime ago, I had written an affirmation about having a personal relationship with three of my top spiritual mentors and role models. I assumed this goal would take up to ten years to materialize because it seemed so far-fetched. I was sure that it would take me this long just to "earn the right" to even have the relationships.

Nevertheless, I prayed about it, thought about it over and over again and was very emotionally wrapped up in trying to make this happen. I was determined to work towards earning this event, for the hope of it coming to fruition in the future.

"I'm a great believer in luck, and I find the harder I work the more I have of it."

- THOMAS EDISON

107

However, it didn't take ten years. Unexpectedly, I miraculously found myself in a car with two of them, for over an hour, within only three months.

So let me ask you, **Do you think I had anything to do with this event happening or do you think it was just a coincidence?**

2. I was born and raised in England, but at the age of nineteen, I came to Canada for a holiday for about three months. In the last week of my holiday I was invited to an anniversary party. During the party, I found myself sitting on a staircase with another guy, just chatting.

All of a sudden, a girl in a green outfit walked by. When she passed in front of my eyes, it was as though she put me into a trance. My heart-rate shot through the roof and I began to feel really, really strange. My heart was beating in my chest so hard that I thought everyone would hear it. I got up off the stairs and followed her.

She went into the basement where everybody was gathered. I saw her sit down on the floor near the back of the room with some other girls.

My older brother, who lived in Canada, was also in the same room. As soon as I spotted where this girl was sitting, I asked my brother if he could see the girl in the green outfit at the back of the room. He said, "Yes, why?" I said to him, "I'm going to marry her." The crazy thing was, we hadn't even met yet.

I absolutely shocked my brother when I told him I needed his help to talk to her father. I wanted to suggest an arranged marriage for the two of us if she agreed. Arranged marriages were a common thing in our Indian culture.

He said he would talk to her father in the next few days, but I was not about to wait that long. That night, I got a chance to find out her name. I talked to her for about five minutes but that was all.

The next day I found myself sitting in a rocking chair listening to Paul Anka love songs and praying to God, which was strange at the time because I was a devout atheist. I prayed a simple, but very emotional prayer; I promised God that I would believe in him if he helped me marry this girl.

"Speech is the mirror of the mind."

- SENECA

> *"What lies behind us and what lies before us are tiny matters compared to what lies within us."*
>
> - RALPH WALDO EMERSON

For the next few hours all I could do was think about this girl and listen to love songs. I was love struck.

All of a sudden, the phone rang. The caller was a friend of the girl in green; she had also been at the party that night. She was asking me for a double-date. I asked her what other girl would be joining us. She told me that it would be Rani. That was the name of the girl in green.

I almost had a heart-attack, but I agreed. Five minutes after I put the phone down, the phone rang again. This time it was Rani herself.

Now I really thought I was going to have a heart-attack. She asked me if I got a call from her friend and what she had said to me. I told Rani I only agreed to go on the double-date because I had found out that she was also going.

Surprisingly to me, she said, "The only reason I was going, was because I found out that you were going." Now I was definitely sure I was having a heart-attack. I suggested to her that we cancel the double-date and go on a date by ourselves. She agreed.

We met the very next day and spent the whole day together. We shared so much about ourselves. It was an amazing day.

That night, as she went back to her house, I went to my brother's place. When I got there, I went straight to the phone. I called her and asked her how she was doing and then I said to her, "So, do you want to get married?" and she replied, "Yes."

...I know it sounds crazy, but that's exactly what happened and by my twentieth birthday we were married! Today we have been married for twenty-two years and have two boys.

... By the way, I'm no longer an atheist.

So let me ask you again, **Do you think I had anything to do with the outcome of this event or do you think it was just another coincidence?**

> *"The secret to developing the best relationships, is to leave your world and join them in theirs."*
>
> - TERRY GOGNA

> *"I pack my trunk, embrace my friends, embark on the sea, and at last wake up in Naples, and there beside me is the Stern fact, the Sad Self, unrelenting, identical, that I fled from."*
>
> - RALPH WALDO EMERSON

3. A few years ago I was going through a very tough time personally. Everything around me was great: family, marriage, kids; it was just me. I was trying to build my business and I was having a very tough time staying focused. I couldn't get myself to do the things I knew I should be doing. I would get so distracted. I felt like there was something wrong with me. Besides the fact that I had very bad discipline, I also had some really bad habits that I was not proud of; losing my temper was one of them and the rest were mostly spiritual in nature.

I was having a very hard time understanding my role in this world that I was in. I had so many questions spinning around in my head all the time and everybody I asked had absolutely no clue about the answers. The surprising thing was, most of them weren't even bothered and the ones who did answer my questions just repeated stuff they had read, but didn't even understand.

My questions were of this nature: Where did I come from? What am I supposed to be doing on this earth? Where am I going when I die? Why is this earth so messed up? Why have so many good people died so tragically while the bad are living it up? Why does a little kid get cancer? Where is God? Why is he hiding? If he is so powerful, why doesn't he fix all the problems on this Earth? If God made me on purpose, then why did he make me like this?

"A man is not idle because he is absorbed in thought. There is a visible labor and there is an invisible labor."

- VICTOR HUGO

I hated my habits. I wanted to achieve great things, but could not get myself to stay focused and do what I was supposed to be doing. I was so angry at God, every night I would pray to God and curse him at the same time because he wouldn't show his face and give me the answers. "Why aren't you showing your face? What kind of joke is this?" I would repeatedly ask him.

Sometime over the next year, I decided to try and make some cold-calls out of the phonebook for my business. I was going to start at the A's, when all of a sudden I had a weird thought/voice in my head. I heard, "I can't help you if you start at the A's." So I closed the book and just opened it to any page and started calling. I did this for a number of days and was able to set up some appointments.

"Your most valuable lessons will be learned in the most unexpected places, from the least expected people, at the worst of times."

- TERRY GOGNA

One of the appointments that I set up was with a guy in the IT industry. At the beginning of our appointment I asked him, "By the way, what else do you do other than IT?" He said he was a Reverend on the weekends. "Wow," I said. "You've got to be kidding. You know, I've always wondered what happens to you after you die." He started laughing. He got up and pulled a book off his shelf and handed it to me. "When you get a chance, why don't you read this and tell me what you think of the content?" I said, "Sure, I'll check it out, thanks." And we proceeded with our business meeting.

To make a long story short, the great Reverend Mitch Dixon, whom I met by some fluke or miracle, actually ended up changing my whole life. Through the books he encouraged me to read and the hours he spent, personally teaching me, all my spiritual questions were answered logically.

114

So let me ask you once again...

Do you think I had anything to do with this event happening or do you think it was still just another coincidence?

"Everything comes to him who hustles while he waits."

- THOMAS A. EDISON

Chapter 12

There Is No Such Thing As A Secure Job Or Business, There Are Only "Secure" People

"Most powerful is he who has himself in his own power."

- SENECA

A few years ago, I was applying for a job in the "employment-recruiting industry" and I was asked to bring in a resume of my previous work experience. When I arrived at this particular company's office, the receptionist asked me for my resume. I told her that I had never had a job; I had been running my own business for the last ten years, and that was why I didn't have a resume. She wasn't very pleased with my answer. Still, she told me to take a seat and wait for the owner of the company to call me in.

The owner of the recruiting firm was a very professional and pleasant lady. However, she asked me the same question, "Where's your resume?" I told her the same story. I could see that she wasn't very impressed with my answer; seeing her roll her eyes kind of gave that away. But she was nice about it and continued with the interview anyway.

She asked me, "So, why are you looking for a job in this industry and why should I hire you?"

I leaned forward and began to explain in point form...

- I'm looking for a career change
- I've researched this industry & I know you can make a lot of money in it
- I'm not shy
- People don't intimidate me no matter how much money they make
- I can talk to anyone on the phone
- I can take rejection
- I've read a lot of personal growth and leadership books
- I don't have a problem with my self-esteem
- I don't need someone to motivate me

- I set goals for everything I do
- I'm totally focused and I don't like wasting my time with people that don't want to win
- I'm not just looking for a company to work for, I'm looking for a coach
- I'm looking for someone to train me and teach me exactly how to make a lot of money in this industry
- I know that you don't have to hire me, but I'm either going to be working for you or for your competition
- So now that I've told you about myself I'd like to ask you, "What's good about your company and why should I work for you?"

"Everything is worth what its purchaser will pay for it."

- PUBLILIUS SYRUS

She began to tell me about her company. Then she told me she would call me after speaking with her business partner to let me know if they would be interested in hiring me.

Two hours later I got a call; I got the job.

The owner of this employment agency knew that **there is no such thing as a secure job or business, there are only secure people** and when you find one, you do whatever you have to, to keep them on your team.

A True Example of a "Secure" Person

My father was born in India in the year 1929. He was the second oldest of eight siblings and was married at the age of sixteen. At the age of twenty-four he left India and went to England via cruise-ship.

In England his first job was as a hard labourer in a metal-window manufacturing plant and he lived in a house with three other men. One of the men that he lived with advised my Dad to start his own business. He reminded him, "You didn't come to England to work in a factory."

My Dad purchased a car and then took his drivers test (yes, in that order). He then started selling clothes door-to-door, out of his car, on the weekends. Eventually he made enough money to buy a house. Then my Mom joined him in England. Within a few short years, there were six of us kids and my parents living in the house.

My Dad's younger brother was the next person to come to England from India. He became my Dad's business partner and together they started building their businesses. They called themselves "Gogna Brothers" and everyone in town knew who they were. They owned a number of shops & houses and were very successful. The reason I'm telling you this story is because of what I discovered about my Dad when I was just fourteen-years-old.

I went with my Dad to buy some goods at a wholesale sports-clothing supplier. On the way out, the man asked my Dad for a cheque for thirteen-hundred pounds, about twenty-six-hundred Canadian dollars. My Dad took his cheque book out and gave it to the man and said, "There you go, you write it." I was watching and thought that it was quite strange. The man wrote the cheque and my Dad looked at it and said, "that's ok" and signed it. When I got in the car, I asked him why he didn't write the cheque. His answer *blew me away,* because he told me he didn't know how to read or write English! He could only understand the numbers on the cheque.

All these years, all this success and he had fooled everyone, including his own kids. How he did it amazes me, but he did it. Now that's a truly "secure" person; no excuses, only action and results.

"Action is eloquence."

- WILLIAM SHAKESPEARE

121

> *"A person who has knowledge but no confidence has the same value as a person who knows nothing."*
>
> - TERRY GOGNA

What Exactly is a "Secure" Person?

A "secure" person is a person of extreme confidence and value in the eyes of others.

The greater the value, the more secure the person.

An adequate amount of knowledge and skill are always needed. However, every employer's dream is to find that hungry, driven, passionate, teachable person, with the right attitude and confidence.

A person who has knowledge but no confidence has the same value as a person who knows nothing.

How do you increase your confidence?
By increasing your value.

How do you increase your value?
There are three ways:

Three Ways To Increase Your Value:

1. If you maintain an attitude of, always being hungry to learn, you will naturally increase your value.

2. Every time you learn a new skill you will increase your value.

3. Every time you invest time and effort, into your personal development, you will increase your value more than anything else, because an increase in emotional and mental strength will accelerate your learning in all other areas.

Two Examples:

1. A person that has developed a high level of emotional and mental strength will not panic in stressful times. They are very valuable people to have on a team.

2. A person that has developed a high level of emotional and mental strength understands and accepts that in every facet of learning, there will always be a "Victory Valley Experience" that the learner must go through in order to succeed.

"Try to become not a man of success, but rather to become a man of value."

- ALBERT EINSTEIN

123

"Victory belongs to the most persevering."

- NAPOLEON BONAPARTE

When we begin to learn something new, like a new language for example, we are usually excited, and for two reasons. First, because it's new and secondly, because the initial content that we were given to learn was actually easy.

The advanced learner knows that it is easy because we are only learning light content at the start. He understands that this *easy* feeling is temporary and we had better be prepared for what's about to come.

In a very short period of time, the learner will hit their "Victory Valley Experience." This is where they are pushed to their limits. They will fail many times. They will feel totally frustrated and discouraged and will think seriously about whether they should continue learning or just quit.

The advanced learner knows that they MUST develop a dogged, tenacious mindset in order to get themselves through their "Victory Valley" and back onto the road where they can start to enjoy their learning again.

Advanced Learners Mindset

1. They accept the "Victory Valley Experience" as a mandatory process of ALL learning.

2. They expect it and are prepared for it when it comes.

3. They know that when they begin to feel frustrated and discouraged it is not a reason to quit learning, but a sign of progress.

4. They understand that their time in "Victory Valley" is ALWAYS temporary. They will only be there until they learn what they need to learn and then they will be out. The pain will pass.

5. They believe that as long as they chase their true passion, their mission, their purpose in life, then by divine intervention, they will be protected until they accomplish that, which they were born to accomplish.

"If you are going through hell, keep going."

- WINSTON CHURCHILL

125

> *"Anyone can hold the helm when the sea is calm."*
>
> - Publilius Syrus

Most people hate getting flu shots, but will put themselves through the pain of getting the shot because they know the pain will only last about one second and then it's over for another year.

Most people hate going to the dentist, but will put themselves through the pain of getting their teeth cleaned because they know the pain and frustration will only last about thirty minutes and then it's over for another six months.

Most novice learners give up and quit when frustration and discouragement come their way. Many actually believe the struggle to be a sign from God that they shouldn't go any further.

However, knowing that every "Victory Valley Experience" has a time-limit, empowers ADVANCED learners to persevere.

In all facets of learning there will be many "Victory Valley Experiences." And just like in the sport of running, as long as you hang in there, your "second-wind" is always just around the corner.

Here are just a few of the areas in which you can look forward to growing when you read and listen to personal growth books and CDs:

-How to be a valuable team player
-How to work with different personalities
-How to set goals
-How to develop the leader within you
-How to develop the leaders around you
-How to increase your confidence
-How to empower others
-How to improve your communication skills
-How to have better relationships with your family, friends and peers
-How to improve your discipline
-How to handle rejection
-How to develop the strength to overcome your fears
-How to handle adversity in your life
-Secrets of the wealthy
-How to coach and mentor others
-How to develop more courage
-How to become the person you know you can be
-Time management
-Learning how successful people think
-Dressing for success
-Emotional intelligence
-Developing success habits

"I will prepare and someday my chance will come."

- ABRAHAM LINCOLN

> *"I not only use all the brains that I have, but all that I can borrow."*
>
> - WOODROW WILSON

-How to get yourself motivated & keep yourself there
-How to improve your performance at work and in business
-Learning the difference between management & leadership
-Little -voice management
-Developing mental toughness
-How to prevent procrastination in all areas of your life
-Developing a servanthood character
-Learning the lessons of history from great men & women
-Wealth creation
-Problem solving
-Knowing what made great people great

When you read personal growth books you tend to start thinking about ways you can improve yourself as a human being.

The less you read, the less you are aware of your own behaviour.

The thoughts in your head are either positive or negative. The longer you dwell on any particular one, the more you will be influenced to act upon it. The actions that you carry out repeatedly become habits and it is ONLY your habits that determine your future.

The more you read daily, the more positive your thoughts will be and the tougher your mind will get. This mental strength will enable you to kick out and block any negative thoughts that try to enter your mind. This process of reading daily will eventually lead to an increase in self-discipline and willpower.

You will find that all strong leaders made time in their early years to read success-oriented positive books. These people have developed, over the years, a certain mindset; they are able to see things differently than the average person. They have learned how, not to panic in unexpected situations of stress. Because of their emotional strength they attract people and opportunities, like magnets.

"A room without books is like a body without a soul."

- CICERO

129

"Only the educated are free."

- EPICTETUS

Anais Nin said, **"We see the world, not as it is, but as we are."**

Before I started reading books and listening to CDs on personal growth, I always struggled with a lack of self-confidence. I was so shy that when I got on a bus or a train I wouldn't even lift my head. I always felt that everyone was looking at me. When I walked, I would just look down at the floor or out of the window, but I would dare not look up at "all these people looking at me."

In particular, I remember one day when I was walking towards an office building at lunch-time. There were a lot of people sitting on some concrete steps outside the building eating their lunch. As I walked towards the building I was petrified, again thinking that all these people were all looking at me as I walked towards the main doors of the building.

After reading and listening to many books and CDs, I finally overcame my lack of confidence in this area. I learned that no one is watching me; instead, they are busy thinking about themselves.

I proved this to myself totally, without a doubt, by simply raising my head and looking into the eyes of each of the people that I thought that were looking at me. I tried it and it blew my mind; it was actually quite hilarious.

As I looked into their eyes, they would immediately stop looking at me and either look to the floor or out of the window. Every single one of them turned away. My God, they were all shy just like me.

The exact same thing happened with the people sitting on the concrete steps outside of the office building. As I walked towards them, I lifted my head and looked straight into their eyes. Every single person I looked at turned their head away, not one person was looking at me. I felt as though I was finally freed from this emotional captivity. I was totally exhilarated.

I had made it all up in my head. Every time I was in a crowd of people, I automatically assumed that they all knew one another and were collaborating with each other to look at me and judge me.

"Desultory reading is delightful, but to be beneficial, our reading must be carefully directed."

- SENECA

> *"Success is to be measured not so much by the position that one has reached in life, as by the obstacles which he has overcome."*
>
> - BOOKER T. WASHINGTON

This was exactly where my fear was coming from. I was totally wrong. They were not together. They were all individuals just sitting or standing close to each other. That's it. No collaboration or group judgment was taking place.

It changed my whole life. I totally misread the picture. My wrong belief was causing me to act in this shy way. But once I discovered that my belief was wrong, I was freed from this shyness. I was totally empowered.

Today I regularly speak to audiences of 500 to 1000 people at a time and I am able to do it comfortably, simply because I look at them all as just individuals who want to grow and not as a crowd collaborating with each other to judge me.

By the way, after reading so many books, I was able to discover for myself where exactly this belief of "crowds judging me" actually came from.

It was back when I was in high-school. I was twelve-years-old and I was walking towards the main doors at the front of the school. About five floors up, there were a number of boys that were looking out of the windows, shouting and making rude gestures "together as a group" at different boys in the same area as I was walking. When one of them saw me, knowing my name, he shouted out loud, "Hey guys, look at how Gogna's walking, he's walking like a duck!" and they all laughed together. Even people in the car park were now looking at me. EVERYONE, I assumed, was looking at me. They were making fun of me because my school bag was bouncing around on my back as I was walking fast.

I can remember the day as though it was yesterday. It wasn't the comment that affected me, it was the fact that all these people were looking at me and supposedly judging me. I was so emotionally affected by this experience that I carried it, unknowingly, for almost twenty-five-years after it happened. I didn't even realize it was embedded deep in my subconscious mind and had been affecting my behaviour, until I started reading personal growth books.

"I cannot live without books."

- THOMAS JEFFERSON

133

"The aim of life is self-development. To realize one's nature perfectly – that is what each of us is here for."

- OSCAR WILDE

When my younger son was nine years of age, I remember taking him to school one day and as he got out of the car I decided to just watch him for a while to see how he behaved with the other children in the playground. I was very disappointed because I noticed that he would follow the other kids everywhere they went as though he had no say in anything. His lack of confidence was so apparent by his body language. He reminded me of myself when I was his age and how I did not enjoy school at all because my self-confidence was so low.

I decided to pay my son to read positive personal growth books. I made a deal with him that if he finished a book within two weeks I would pay him $10 and if he finished it within one, I would pay him $20. However, if he didn't finish the book within two weeks he would be paid nothing and he would not get to watch any television until the book was finished. I had no choice but to make sure he read these books. I did not want him to suffer through high-school lacking confidence like I did.

Two years later, all parents of the children at Cherokee Public School were invited to a graduation ceremony for the seniors of the school. My son was now eleven years of age and this was his last year at the school.

At the ceremony, the principal recognized many students for their achievements throughout the year. Each one was invited up on stage to collect their certificates. Sadly, and to my surprise, my son was not one of them.

The principal then held up a gold plated wooden plaque and said, "Each year a very special senior student is awarded this 'Principal's Award for Student Leadership' plaque. It goes to the student that exemplifies character, leadership, social skills, discipline and excellence in all facets of their work. This student is the number one role model of the year for all senior students. Please join me in congratulating Aaron Gogna for achieving this distinguished award." I almost fell off my chair. My wife and I were absolutely amazed and so proud.

"Men are generally more careful of the breed of their horses and dogs than of their children."

- WILLIAM PENN

> *"I have never let my schooling interfere with my education."*
>
> - Mark Twain

However, the thing that blew me away the most, was what happened next.

My son had to make a speech and as he was about to begin, he noticed that the microphone was a little lower than it should have been because it was on the floor and not on the stage. With absolute confidence he got off the stage, grabbed the microphone stand and placed it on the stage in front of him. That was the moment I knew my son finally achieved the level of confidence and leadership that any parent would dream that their son would reach. This, I believe, is a true testament to the awesome power of personal growth books.

A "secure" person always has a formula that they use to get themselves to do what they need to do when they just don't feel like doing it.

A secure person understands and accepts that there will be many times during the course of their life where they will feel at sometime or another, mentally exhausted, discouraged and possibly, even heartbroken, when life is just not going the way that they expected it to go.

The secure person knows that they have to accept the challenges of life as a part of the journey. They are also well aware that they had better have a strategic plan to get themselves up when they are down and to get themselves to do what they need to, when they just don't feel like doing it.

They know they must get up as quickly as possible because the longer they stay down, the harder it will be for them to get back on track again.

A pilot once told me that if any plane crashes, the goal of the airline is to get as many of their pilots back up in the air as quickly as possible before inertia sets in and a pilot is filled with a fear of flying.

Many people look at successful secure people from their outside appearance and make comments like:

"If he can do it, so can I."

"I'm so much more talented than he is; I'm going to break his record."

> *"Things do not change, we change."*
>
> - HENRY DAVID THOREAU

"The highest reward for man's toil is not what he gets for it, but what he becomes by it."

- JOHN RUSKIN

We cannot see what is on the inside of a person. We cannot see their level of commitment, drive, resilience, focus, discipline, habits, consistency, passion, heart or whatever else there may be deep inside of them that is actually responsible for creating who they are and their success.

By looking at a person from the outside, we can only see how they are dressed, how they walk and how they talk.

You will only be successful if you have inside of you, the things that successful people have inside of them. Otherwise, you will not make it like they did. Even though you have such great "outside" talents, you will not be successful until you develop the "true causes" of success that they have developed inside of them.

I remember so many times when I used to sit in my office. I had pictures of my dreams all over the walls; I had six month, one year and three year goals written on cards and pinned onto my notice board. My desk was spotless, paperwork all done, full stomach, water on my table, comfortable chair, phone in front of me, but I could not get myself to pick up the phone to make prospecting calls for my business. I was paralyzed by "something" but I didn't know what it was. I was actually excellent at making calls, when I did them. However, getting myself to do it consistently was the issue.

I would visualize a little green man, in the corner of my room snickering at the fact that I was procrastinating. I would hear him say, "Do you know that 'such and such' TV show is on right now? You love that show. Forget your calls tonight and do them tomorrow." Sometimes he would say, "It's getting late. Why don't you call it a night and lie down on your nice, warm, comfy bed; it'll feel great." Other times he would just say, "Why don't you get yourself a nice cold drink from the fridge and then get started?" Knowing that if I left my room, making calls that night was over.

Every time I listened to him and gave up on making my calls, I would then hear as I'm leaving my office, "I got you again!" followed by laughter. This went on for so long. I thought there was something wrong with me because I just couldn't get myself to do what I needed to do, to create a better future for myself.

"If people knew how hard I work to gain mastery, it wouldn't seem so wonderful at all."

- MICHELANGELO BUONARROTI

"Nature herself has never attempted to effect great changes rapidly."

- QUINTILIAN

Even though I had such a hard time with this, I wasn't about to give up on my dreams. I was determined that one day, no matter how long it took, I would discover the way to overcome this challenge in my life... and I did.

<u>Strategic Formulas</u> for getting yourself to do what you need to do, when you just don't feel like doing it:

1. Your Dream
2. Your Pain
3. Your Consequence
4. Your Accountability
5. Your Cause
6. Your Hero
7. Your Gladiator Statement
8. Your Finest Hour
9. Your Dialogue with God
10. Your Positive Past

These ten formulas are different mindsets and practices that you can apply in order to get yourself to do the things that you need to do, to succeed.

For example, let's say you just started a part-time business outside of your full-time job. You want to make more money to get out of debt and have a better lifestyle, but even though you need and want to make the money, you somehow find it difficult to get yourself motivated enough to actually do the work consistently. Yet you know you must do it, in order to be successful.

Even though it sounds crazy, the motivation of making more money to get yourself out of debt and have a better lifestyle for your family, on it's own, is just simply not enough; something is missing. Something else is needed to get yourself to do, what you need to do.

It's like this; say you want to give more money to charity, but even though this is a great goal, it is just not motivating you enough to get the work done to make the money to give to charity. So you adopt a different mindset. Instead, you focus on something else that empowers you. Let's say it's a Mercedes 500SL. The chance of having a car like this pumps you up so much that you are now off the couch and working consistently at building your business.

"Strong reasons make strong actions."

- WILLIAM SHAKESPEARE

141

"A man's mind, once stretched by a new idea, never regains its original dimensions."

- OLIVER WENDELL HOLMES

You put up pictures of your dream car everywhere, you test-drive it and you constantly visualize yourself owning and driving it.

Do you think that, by the time you can afford to get your Mercedes 500SL, you will also be in a position to give more money away to charity? Of course you will. You will accomplish both dreams by simply applying a formula that changed your mindset.

The reason so many people don't do this is because they have been programmed by guilt. They feel that their priorities ought to be motivation enough. They say things like, "I can't think about material things like cars; it's wrong, charity is more important than cars." Yet they do nothing and fail at both.

The secret lies in discovering that which "stirs your soul," discovering the passion within. Once you discover it, all that's left, is to then chase it with everything you've got. By doing this, you will get everything else that is important to you as well.

Formula 1: Your Dream

This formula is about keeping your dream in front of you at all times. Putting up pictures of what you want. Touching, smelling and experiencing your dream. If it's a new car, go and test-drive it. If it's a new home, go and visit model homes.

Many people get energized and back on track really fast by simply going out and experiencing the dreams that they want. Pictures are great, but the real power comes from the experience. When you experience that special dream it will enter your heart and stir your soul to the point that nothing will stop you from achieving it.

If you feel strongly that you have discovered your dream and yet you still lack power to act, you are mistaken. You have not discovered your dream yet; keep searching. **You may have to look in the areas of your life that you would not normally look into.**

If this formula causes you to act and do what you need to, mission accomplished. You're on track and you probably don't need any of the other formulas.

"Security is mostly a superstition. It does not exist in nature... Life is either a daring adventure or nothing."

- HELEN KELLER

However, if it's not getting you to do what you need to, then you may seriously have to consider adopting one of the other formulas in addition to this.

Formula 2: Your Pain

If focusing on your dream is not empowering you to act, then maybe the answer lies in focusing on your pain. Maybe at this time in your life the power and the passion that will cause you to act when you don't feel like acting, is somehow attached to your pain.

Maybe you need to think seriously about what you don't want in your life.

By the way, it is a dangerous practice to use this formula for a long period of time because you will attract that which you "think about" and "feel about" all the time. Use this formula only as a catalyst to get you up and moving and then focus on the positive aspects of that which you will receive upon relieving your pain.

For example, if you are thinking, "I hate my job, I want to quit it as soon as I can," then ask yourself, "What is it that you want to do instead?" And then focus on that.

Formula 3: Your Consequence

Why is it that no matter how late we go to bed and no matter how rotten we feel in the morning, we still manage to get ourselves out of bed and off to work? The answer is CONSEQUENCE. We have something to lose **immediately** if we don't go to work. That something is a paycheck.

The fear of immediate loss, especially a paycheck, will make us do, that which we really don't want to.

One way that you can get yourself to do what you need to, is to **create some sort of immediate consequence.**

For example:

If you have young children, tell them that when you do "such and such" you will take them out for pizza but until you do it, you cannot take them. You have now created an immediate consequence because if you don't do what you said you were going to do, you will not only disappoint yourself but more importantly, your children.

"If you would not be forgotten as soon as you are dead and rotten, either write something worth reading or do things worth the writing."

- BENJAMIN FRANKLIN

"If a man takes no thought about what is distant, he will find sorrow near at hand."

- CONFUCIUS

Another example is to give someone close to you, $200 CASH and tell them that if you don't get "such and such" done, by a specific date that you have set, they can keep the money.

A few years ago, my son came to me and told me that he decided that he did not want to go to University. I did not fight him on his decision, but instead I began to explain to him the reality of the process I had to follow at the employment agency, in order to find the right person quickly for a job opening that we were given. Here is the process I explained:

1. Because we had over 100 people for most of the job openings we had to first filter out all those who did not have degrees. No matter how good they were, we couldn't even talk to them because we simply did not have the time.

The degree demonstrates to an employer that you have discipline, focus, organizational skills, determination to finish a long-term task and the willpower to stay with something even though you did not get paid for your efforts at the time.

2. We then eliminated all those who had no experience.

3. We then eliminated all those who had less than two years experience

4. We then eliminated all those who were over-qualified for the job; usually those over fifty.

Now we had a small enough number of people that we could actually call-in and personally interview as potentials to fill the job.

After explaining this to him I then grabbed a couple of newspapers and said to him, "Okay, let's assume you have finished school right now and you want to get a job. Let's look in the newspaper and see exactly what kind of jobs that you would actually qualify for, considering you have no other job experience other than McDonalds and no degree."

"What we think, or what we know, or what we believe is, in the end, of little consequence. The only consequence is what we do."

- JOHN RUSKIN

I began to read through the job listings that did not require a degree or any specialized education. As I read them he replied with a "yes" or a "no" depending on whether he would want this kind of job for himself:

Courier driver? – "NO"
Truck driver? – "NO"
Warehouse worker? – "NO"
Factory worker? – "NO"
Retail sales clerk? – "NO"
Street sales? – "NO"
Construction worker? – "NO"
Telemarketing? – "NO"
Gas station attendant? – "NO"
Waiter? – "NO"
Cleaner? –"NO"
Nanny? – "NO, that's enough Dad, what about all the good jobs?" He asked.

"Are you talking about these career jobs?" I asked, as I pointed to the management/career opportunity job listings. He said, "Yes, those are the ones."

I began to read them out as well and every one of them required either a degree or a degree & a minimum of two years experience.

"OK Dad, I get your point," my son said.

The consequences of not having a degree motivated my son enough to get back on track with his studies and focus on getting into University.

By the way, he qualified with an 88.8% average and got into the "Business Management Co-op Program" at the University of Toronto.

Formula 4: Your Accountability

If you can't do what you need to do for yourself, do it for someone else.

Most people will always go that extra mile and do more for someone else who is counting on them rather than simply stretch for themselves.

If you tell someone that you are going to do something, will you quit or will you keep trying until you get it done?

This is a very powerful formula; finding someone to be accountable to, telling them what you are planning on doing and by when you are planning on doing it and then getting to work.

"We cannot always build the future for our youth, but we can build our youth for the future."

- FRANKLIN D. ROOSEVELT

You'll be absolutely amazed at how fast you'll get things done if you are accountable to someone that you respect because now your word is on the line.

Personal Success Coach

In this highly competitive age that we live in, many success-oriented people have personal success coaches, to whom they pay a monthly fee, in order to have someone they can be accountable to on a professional level.

The number one purpose of the coach is to help them do what they know they can do, but for some reason, won't do on their own.

Benefits of Being Coached

1. People who are being coached are learning not just from their own experiences, but from the personal experiences of their coach. Being coached will enable them to achieve success earlier than they are capable of achieving alone. It takes a lot less time to find a coach than to acquire the knowledge and understanding that the coach already has.

2. Accountability to a coach always increases personal performance and results.

3. "Focus" always creates blindness in other areas. The coach can help you to see the bigger picture and stay on track because he/she is not emotionally involved in the areas of your life about which you are being coached in.

4. The coach will help you to discover your unique ability.

5. The coach will help you to identify and overcome the obstacles that are preventing you from achieving the success you want.

6. If you are already working hard but your life is not changing as fast as you would like it to change, a coach will help you to see your life from a different perspective, which in turn will help you to be more effective. Working even harder is not usually the solution; working smarter is the key.

"Our chief want in life is somebody who shall make us do what we can."

- RALPH WALDO EMERSON

"If a writer wrote merely for his time, I would have to break my pen and throw it away."

- VICTOR HUGO

When is the Right Time to get a Coach?

The goal of a coach is to get you to the top of your "game" and keep you there.

If you are near the bottom, the coach will help you get to the top. If you are already at the top, the coach will help you to stay at the top.

So many more people would achieve their dreams if they had only made the decision to invest in a personal success coach.

And...

So many fortunes would not have been lost if the person who was at the top of their game, had also humbled themselves and invested in a coach while they were at the top.

Formula 5: Your Cause

Oscar Schindler is portrayed, in the movie "Schindler's List," as a German capitalist. His only motivation in life was to simply make money and enjoy the trappings of material success. As he made more and more money he was able to hire more employees for his company, which then helped him to make even more money.

As he was building his wealth, things around him started to drastically change because of the war. The Nazis started exterminating all the Jewish people in the area. All of Schindler's employees were Jewish and they were the only ones that were not killed because they worked for his company, which supposedly made ammunition for the Nazis.

Schindler started to feel great compassion for his employees and realized that they were only alive because of him. His compassion started to drive his actions and as a result, he started to hire more people, even though he didn't need them, just to save them from being killed.

"The world is my country, all mankind are my brethren, and to do good is my religion."

- THOMAS PAINE

"Every artist dips his brush in his own soul and paints his own nature, into his pictures."

- HENRY WARD BEECHER

He then started taking money out of his company, any way he could and literally began to buy Jews with his money. He bribed the Nazis with money in exchange for Jews that were on their way to the gas chambers. He told them that he needed these people for his company.

At the end of the movie there is a very emotional scene where Oscar Schindler is crying, saying, "I should have done more. If I had only made more money I could have saved one more person."

His motivation changed from, making money for "status and good living," to **making money for a cause**. The cause was so important to him that he literally bankrupted himself to save the lives of over 1100 Jews.

If you cannot get yourself to do what you need to do by focusing on what you are currently focusing on, then maybe you need to think seriously about a cause that you believe in. Perhaps this is where your power will come from to get yourself to do what you need to.

How many times do we hear ourselves praying like this,

"Dear God,
please help me with my business
please help me with my health
please help me with my finances
please help me with my job
please help me with my kids
please help me with my marriage
please help me with my..."

We have a "grocery list" of things that we would like God to help us with.

How do you think God would react to a prayer like this?

"Dear God, thank you for everything in my life, the good and also the bad. God, there is only one thing that I would like from you and that is to know what I can do for you. I would like to know how I can make your life easier. What is it that I can do to put a smile on your face? What can I do to give you back some joy for creating me? I don't need anything other than to know what I can do for you. How can I help you? Please tell me what is on your mind and in your heart. How can I help you accomplish your heart's desire?"

"Only a life lived for others is a life worthwhile."

- ALBERT EINSTEIN

If you were God and you heard someone praying to you like this, how would you react?

If you truly believe that by being successful in what you are doing will make this world a better place, which in turn will warm God's heart to the point of shedding tears of joy, would you still hesitate to do that, which you know you need to.

Formula 6: Your Hero

Do you have a hero? Is there someone that you deeply respect, admire and look up to? If you do, think about the accomplishments of your hero. Think about the struggles your hero has persevered through. Think about the pain your hero has experienced.

The more you admire and love your hero, the more you will feel your hero's pain as you internalize their struggle through their story of how they accomplished their goal.

156

Put up pictures of your hero in times of victory; more importantly, find pictures of your hero during their greatest struggles.

When you internalize the amount of pain and sorrow your hero experienced as he struggled and persevered to accomplish his goal/mission, you will come to the realization that your pain, in comparison, is quite insignificant. This realization will empower you to make no excuses and to do what you need to.

Your hero does not necessarily need to be someone with whom you have had a personal relationship. They could be anyone you admire deeply: Martin Luther King Jr., Gandhi, Harriet Tubman, William Wallace, Sir Winston Churchill, Abraham Lincoln or any of the great spiritual founders and saints of the different religions of the world.

"It is the way we react to circumstances that determines our feelings."

- DALE CARNEGIE

Formula 7:
Your "Gladiator Statement"

A totally "secure" person knows exactly who they are, where they have come from and where they are going. In the film, "Gladiator," there is an incredible part where the Gladiator was asked by the emperor, "Who are you? Tell me your name." Upon removing his mask, the Gladiator replied with absolutely no hesitancy or doubt in his words:

"My name is
Maximus Decimus Meridius;
Commander of the Armies of the North;
General of the Felix Legion;
Loyal servant to the true emperor, Marcus Aurelius;
Father to a murdered son;
Husband to a murdered wife;
And I will have my vengeance, in this life or the next."

The Gladiator knew exactly who he was; his passion and purpose were burning in every part of his being.

Who you are is not what you do as a job or profession. As you personally grow, you will learn more about yourself and about who you really are deep within.

Where you've come from is not as important as where you want to go and where you are being driven to, from the passion within.

"My life is my message."

- MOHANDAS GANDHI

Empower yourself by writing your own personal Gladiator statement.

This is a difficult exercise but well worth doing. It may take many attempts over a long period of time; you are trying to put into words who you are inside and attempting to identify the real passions that are actually driving you.

Your Gladiator statement, once completed, will empower you every time you read it, especially in times of struggle.

So go ahead, give it a shot.

My name is...
I am...

> *"Nothing in the world can take the place of persistence. Talent will not; nothing is more common than unsuccessful men with talent. Genius will not; unrewarded genius is almost a proverb. Education will not; the world is full of educated derelicts. Persistence and determination alone are omnipotent. The slogan 'Press On' has solved and always will solve the problems of the human race."*
>
> - CALVIN COOLIDGE

Formula 8: Your "Finest Hour"

In one of his most famous speeches, Churchill spoke the following:

"The whole fury and might of the enemy must very soon be turned on us. Hitler knows that he will have to break us in this island or lose the war. If we can stand up to him, all Europe may be free, and the life of the world may move forward into broad, sunlit uplands; but if we fail, then the whole world, including the United States, and all that we have known and cared for, will sink into the abyss of a new dark age made more sinister, and perhaps more protracted, by the lights of a perverted science. Let us therefore brace ourselves to our duty and so bear ourselves that if the British Empire and its Commonwealth last for a thousand years, men will say, **'This was their Finest Hour.'**"

If you haven't already experienced it, your "Finest Hour" will be a time in your life when you are struggling greatly, needing every last bit of hope to hold onto and at the very last moment when you so desperately need "something" to give you confidence, that "something" will **NOT** arrive.

This will be your Finest Hour. The hour that you decide to hang in a little longer and not quit and just do what you need to anyway. Not because you are empowered to do so, but simply because it's the right thing to do.

In the movie "Cinderella Man," even though James Braddock lost everything and was brought down to his knees by the recession, his Finest Hour was not yet upon him.

Even though the image, "Past Due," a note that the milk man had left, was painfully embedded in his mind because he couldn't even afford milk for his kids, his finest hour was still not yet upon him.

Even though he stopped praying after whispering to his wife, "I'm all prayed out," his Finest Hour was not yet upon him.

James Braddock had promised his eldest son that no matter how bad it got, he would not abandon his kids and make them live somewhere else. His Finest Hour was finally upon him when he came home to an empty dark house.

"The world breaks everyone and afterward many are strong in the broken places. But those that will not break, it kills. It kills the very good and the very gentle and the very brave impartially. If you are none of these, you can be sure it will kill you too, but there will be no special hurry."

- ERNEST HEMINGWAY

The heating and the lights were turned off because of non-payment and the kids were gone. His wife had asked her sister if the kids could live there for a while until things got better. She did not know about the promise James made with his eldest son.

Even though James Braddock's spirit was finally broken, he refused to give up. He refused to break the promise he made to his son.

He went to the executives' lounge at the boxing club. Everyone there knew him as an injured boxer. He literally took the hat off his head and begged for money to get his kids back.

This was his Finest Hour. Even though his circumstances couldn't possibly get any worse, James Braddock did not give up, nor did he betray his morals to steal. At the lowest point of his life, he still choose to keep his integrity and his word.

I personally believe that his refusal to give up and to stick with his moral standards was the condition he created for God to bless his life from then onward.

Formula 9: Your Dialogue with God

Your ears, your silence and your patience are the greatest of healers of the sorrowful.

The greatest way to help someone through their struggles is to simply listen to them; listen to their story and to their heart, without talking back.

So many people have a story, that they want to tell. So many people need someone to tell that story to and there is no one that will listen. Everybody is so busy talking that no one has time to listen.

When I was going through some terrible personal times in my life I always felt that I could not really pour my heart out to anyone. I came from a culture that taught you to be a man and handle things yourself and not burden others with your pain. So, as a result I chose never to share my deepest sorrows with anyone. I just kept them inside.

"Your ears, your silence and your patience, are the greatest of healers of the sorrowful."

- TERRY GOGNA

163

"Never to suffer would never to have been blessed."

- EDGAR ALLAN POE

When you have no way of emptying your heart of your pain, your personality changes to accommodate all that which you have locked up inside, how could you possibly be motivated and driven to build a great future when you have to carry such a heavy load?

I had always known about this particular scripture in the Bible:

"Come unto me, all ye that labour and are heavy laden, and I will give you rest."

But I had never dreamt of actually trying to apply it, until one day I heard a voice in my head saying, "Why don't you talk to me?" It seemed weird. I was thinking, why would I share my heart with God? He already knows everything about me. He already knows what I would say before the words come out of my mouth. Pretty useless practice.

Then I heard another voice say, "No I don't"... I started to think, maybe God can choose not to know what we're thinking and not to know how we feel at certain times, so we can actually talk to him and share our heart with him.

I decided to accept this thought and try something a little... I guess some would say, "childish." So, like a little child I pretended to talk to an imaginary friend. I thought, who cares what anyone thinks, I'm not exactly going to tell the world that I'm doing this. Let's just see what happens.

I put on some nice background music and got myself a notepad and pen. I put the date at the top of the page and on the left I wrote "Terry" and next to my name I wrote "Hi God, it's me." Then under my name I wrote "God" and answered what I think God would say if he was actually talking back. It was like I was writing a play. I wrote, "Hello," and then I burst out laughing. I couldn't believe I was doing this but I decided to keep going.

The greatest part about this dialogue was that I could decide how God answered me back. After all, I had the pen. I began to write God's answers back to me as though he was the most caring, most thoughtful, most loving, most forgiving and the wisest person that I could ever imagine myself taking to.

"Do not go where the path may lead, go instead where there is no path and leave a trail."

- RALPH WALDO EMERSON

I decided that, as God, he would have the answers to every question that I could ever think to ask.

I decided that he would be willing to listen to me any time I needed to talk and that when I talked to him, he would listen to me as though he had all the time in the world.

I decided that no matter what I did he would never get angry or hold a grudge against me.

I decided that he was the perfect person I could share my heart with, without being embarrassed.

I started writing the dialogue; my questions and his answers according to what I believed he would say. When I wrote his answers I tried to write as fast as I could, so I didn't have to think too much about his answer.

I continued to do this daily and after about a week I couldn't believe what was happening. It was an absolutely brilliant experience.

This was one of the greatest discoveries of my life. I finally had someone to talk to. The experience was so empowering and life changing that it has now become a part of my life.

Maybe this practice of having a daily dialogue with God will help to get yourself empowered enough to do what you need to.

"The greatest good you can do for another is not just to share your riches, but to reveal to him his own."

- BENJAMIN DESRAELI

Formula 10: Your Positive Past

If you take the time to map out the journey of your life up to now, focused on "bringing back to life" the positive events you have experienced in your past, you will be absolutely amazed at what you will discover.

Start by making a list, as long as possible, of all the memorable things that have happened to you in your life up to today. Include personal successes and experiences. Once you have listed them, put them in chronological order, so each experience is dated and in order from the oldest to the latest event. Make sure you leave a space of one or two lines between each item you list.

"Virtue extends our days; he lives two lives who relives his past with pleasure."

- Marcus Valerius
Martialis

Now, looking at each item, ask yourself, "Did anybody either help you to accomplish this personal success or help make your great experience come true?" You may be quite surprised at the names of the people that come up in your mind. It could actually be someone that you greatly dislike but now you actually appreciate them for coming into your life and making a difference.

Remember, if you see a turtle on a fence, he didn't get there by himself. Men who say they are self-made are selfish men. They refuse to give credit to those who have helped them get to where they are in life.

Now look back at your list and write, in-between each of these positive events, only the significant struggles that you have had in your past that you NO LONGER HAVE. Make sure you put them in the correct place. The date of each event is very important.

It will take time to list all the things that you are attempting to write because you simply won't remember everything that has happened in the past that quickly. So give yourself time.

Every time you look at the "map of your positive past" you will be empowered. It will remind you that your life up to now has been full of great experiences, great successes and great people. It will also prove to you that you will always be able to overcome any challenges that come your way in the future, just like you have overcome them in the past.

Make sure you keep building this map. Every time something special happens in your life, record it with the date and the name of the special people that actually contributed to it becoming a reality.

Remember, because your mind is now focused on looking for the next special event in your life to happen so you can record it, you will actually be attracting more great experiences, more great people and more great successes into your life.

"I do not know what I may appear to the world; but to myself I seem to have been only like a boy playing on the seashore, and diverting myself in now and then finding a smoother pebble or a prettier shell than ordinary, whilst the great ocean of truth lay all undiscovered before me."

- ISAAC NEWTON

169

Wisdom Is The "Application" Of Knowledge

"The wise apply the knowledge they acquire, the intellectuals merely store it."

- TERRY GOGNA

Now that you have read this book I encourage you to do what the "wise" do and not what the "average" will always do. You do not become wise by simply acquiring knowledge. You become wise by *applying* the knowledge you acquire. Be wise and carry out the following:

1. Identify the top three most important things that you have learned from reading this book.

2. Send me an e-mail explaining why you chose these as your top three and how they helped you personally and/or professionally.

"Only when you teach something to someone will you realize how well you truly understand, that which you are teaching."

- TERRY GOGNA

By writing this email you will not only internalize the content you are writing about, but you will also begin to understand it more deeply and with a lot more clarity.

Only when you teach something to someone will you realize how well you truly understand that which are teaching. I am giving you the opportunity to teach it to me through an e-mail.

By the way, I will be publishing some of the best e-mails in my next printing of this book. You will be contacted if yours is selected.

3. Set a date to read this book again exactly one month from today. You will be very surprised at how different you perceive the content from your first reading.

4. Go to **www.pemsystem.com** - Order yourself a "P.E.M. System Planner" and start planning ALL areas of your life, **professionally**.

What Makes The "P.E.M. System" Planner So Unique?

1. PLAN EVERY 5 MINUTES OF YOUR DAY FROM 7:00AM TO MIDNIGHT

2. NO FIXED DATES - STARTS FROM THE DAY YOU WANT IT TO START

3. ENCOURAGES YOU TO MULTI-TASK WITHIN ITS UNIQUE LAYOUT

Terry's Top 7 Recommended Reading List

1. The Dream Giver - Bruce Wilkinson

2. Wild At Heart - John Eldredge

3. You Don't Have To Die To Go To Heaven - Derrick Sweet

4. The Saint, The Surfer And The CEO - Robin Sharma

5. The 21 Indispensable Qualities of a Leader - John C. Maxwell

6. Becoming Unstoppable - Ruben Gonzalez

7. Read & Grow Rich - Burke Hedges